CW00487035

THE BLU

A Concise Post War History of Manchester City

DEAN HAYES

Manchester
The PARRS WOOD PRESS

First published in 1999

THE PARRS WOOD PRESS
St Wilfrid's Enterprise Centre
Royce Road
Manchester M15 5BJ

© Dean Hayes 1999

ISBN: 1 903158 02 8

Cover and book design by Glenn B Fleming
Set in Garamond Book
and printed in Great Britain
by Fretwell Print and Design
Healey Works
Goulbourne Street
Keighley BD21 1PZ

ACKNOWLEDGEMENTS

I should like to express my thanks to the following organisations for their assistance: Manchester City FC; The Association of Football Statisticians; The Football League Ltd; The British Newspaper Library; Manchester Central Reference Library; Bolton Central Library and The Harris Library. Thanks also to the following individuals: Ben Hayes; Iain Price; and Peter Stafford. For the use of photographs, my grateful thanks go to the Lancashire Evening Post, Victor Collinge of the Border Bookshop in Todmorden and Michael Clarke. Thanks also to Andy Searle (Parrs Wood Press) for publishing what is the first book in a series of concise post-war histories on north-west football clubs.

ABOUT THE AUTHOR

Dean Hayes is an experienced freelance sports writer specialising in football and cricket. He was educated at Hayward Grammar School, Bolton and West Midlands College of Physical Education and was a primary shcool headteacher until taking up writing full-time four years ago. Having played as a goalkeeper in the Lancashire Amateur League, he now concentrates solely on playing the summer sport. This former cricket professional, now playing as an amateur, has taken over 2,000 wickets in League Cricket. Dean is married with a son and two step children. This is his thirty-sixth football book to be published and his forty-eighth overall.

Contents

Throughout this book there are statistical records of all Manchester City players who have played in the Football League since 1946-47. See key below.

Name ———————	**ALISON, James**			Signing on Date	
Date and place of birth ——	Peebles 11 October 1923			League appearances	
Clubs played for ————	Manchester City	12.49	19	0	0 — Substitute appearances
	Aldershot	07.52	171	0	9 — League goals

A CONCISE POST WAR
HISTORY OF
MANCHESTER CITY

The Blues

When League football resumed after the war, City were eager to regain First Division status. They had been in the Second Division since 1938, just one season after winning the League Championship for the first time in their history.

The team that started the 1946-47 season was quite a familiar one with players like Frank Swift, Sam Barkas, Les McDowall, Bert Sproston, Alex Herd and Andy Black in the side but Peter Doherty, who had scored 30 goals when City won the League title in 1936-37, had joined Derby County in December 1945 for £7,000. After beating Leicester City 3-0 in the opening match of the season, the Blues lost only two of their first 12 games and between 16 November 1946 and 19 April 1947 were unbeaten in 22 league games. On 3 December 1946, Sam Cowan replaced Wilf Wild, as manager. Wild who had been in charge for 14 years, had been a successful manager with more trophies won under his leadership than any previous City boss. City went to the top of the Second Division table for the first time on New Year's Day with a comfortable 4-0 victory over Fulham. Promotion was gained in May when Burnley were beaten 1-0 at Maine Road but because of the bad winter, postponements meant the season went through until June. Despite dropping a few points, City won the title with 62 points, four more than runners-up Burnley. The club's final match on 14 June 1947, the latest finish to a league season ever experienced by the club, saw them beat Newport County 5-1 with George Smith scoring all City's goals. Welsh international Roy Clarke made his debut for the Blues in this match and was in the middle of playing three

Alex Herd

Signed from Scottish club Hamilton Academicals, Alex Herd had a dramatic entry into English football, for within a little over a year of joining the Blues, he had played in two FA Cup Finals for the club.

He made his City debut in a 1-0 defeat at Blackpool in February 1933 and afterwards became a virtual ever-present in one of the club's greatest-ever teams. He starred in the 1936-37 side which won the League Championship, scoring 15 goals in 32 appearances. A deep-lying inside-forward, he would carry the ball forward before releasing it to send his fellow-strikers Tilson, Doherty and Brook to shoot for goal. Alex Herd's career stretched into wartime football and in 1942 he was capped by Scotland. During the FA Cup competition of 1945-46, Herd netted his only hat-trick for City in a 6-2 win over Barrow. When league football resumed, Herd was still at Maine Road and won a Second Division Championship medal in 1946-47. His son David went on to win honours with Manchester United. Alex Herd left the Blues for Stockport County on a free-transfer in March 1948 and on the last day of the 1950-51 season he turned out alongside his son when they were County's inside-forwards against Hartlepool United.

A Concise Post War History of Manchester City

consecutive games in three different divisions. His last game had been for Cardiff City in the Third Division (South), his debut was in the Second Division and the next match he played for the Blues was in the First Division ! The top of Division Two in 1946-47 read:

	P.	W.	D.	L.	F.	A.	Pts
Manchester City	42	26	10	6	78	35	62
Burnley	42	22	14	6	65	29	58
Birmingham City	42	25	5	12	74	33	55

The club's new status attracted some big crowds to Maine Road, the biggest being 71,364 for the local derby with Manchester United on 28 September 1947. The game was goalless and when

ADCOCK Anthony C.

Bethnal Green	27 February 1963			
Colchester United	02.81	192	18	98
Manchester City	06.87	12	3	5
Northampton Town	01.88	72	0	30
Bradford City	10.89	33	5	6
Northampton Town	01.91	34	1	10
Peterborough United	12.91	107	4	35
Luton Town	08.94	0	2	0
Colchester United	08.95	86	16	28

AIMSON Paul E.

Manchester	3 August 1943			
Manchester City	08.60	16	0	4
York City	07.64	77	0	43
Bury	03.66	30	1	11
Bradford City	09.67	23	01	1
Huddersfield Town	03.68	34	4	13
York City	08.69	133	9	55
Bournemouth	03.73	7	2	2
Colchester United	08.73	3	1	2

ALISON James

Peebles	11 October 1923			
Manchester City	12.49	19	0	0
Aldershot	07.52	171	0	9

ALLEN Clive D.

Stepney	20 May 1961			
Queen's Park Rangers	09.78	43	6	32
Arsenal	06.80	0	0	0
Crystal Palace	08.80	25	0	9
Queen's Park Rangers	06.81	83	4	40
Tottenham Hotspur	08.84	97	8	60
Manchester City	08.89	31	22	16
Chelsea	12.91	15	1	7
West Ham United	03.92	4	0	1

ALLSOP Daniel

Australia	10 August 1978			
Manchester City	08.98	3	21	4

ANDERS Harry

St Helens	28 November 1926			
Preston North End	08.45	69	0.	4
Manchester City	03.53	32	0	4
Port Vale	07.56	3	0	0
Accrington Stanley	06.57	114	0	18
Workington	07.60	7	0	1

ATKINSON Dalian R.

Shrewsbury	21 March 1968			
Ipswich Town	06.85	49	11	18
Sheffield Wednesday	07.89	38	0	10

3

Frank Swift

Frank Swift set the standards for goalkeepers before and after the Second World War. Joining Manchester City from Fleetwood on 21 October 1932, he made his league debut on Christmas Day the following year against Derby County.Beginning with his first full season in the league side in 1934-35, Frank Swift was ever-present for four consecutive seasons and missed only one game in 1938-39. In 1934 he was a member of the successful City side that lifted the FA Cup when they beat Portsmouth 2-1. At half-time, Pompey led 1-0 with Swift conceding that he might have saved the goal had he been wearing gloves ! Fred Tilson hit two second-half goals and on the final whistle, the 19-year-old Swift turned to collect his cap and gloves and fainted ! Afterwards he said 'Fancy a great strapping fellow like me fainting in front of all those people and the King.' Swifty could fool around with the best of them. He often used to make an acrobatic flying dive that would have the crowd roaring even though he knew the ball was going well wide.

In 1935 he made an appearance for The Rest in a trial match against England but it was to be after the war when he played in a full international. He won 19 caps for England, his first against Northern Ireland in 1946 and played in many wartime internationals as well as gaining First and Second Division Championship medals along with that 1934 FA Cup winners' medal.

He had been captain of Manchester City for a couple of seasons, when in Italy in 1948 he became the first goalkeeper to captain England. Frank Swift had enormous hands, with a finger span of almost a foot; he would catch the ball in one hand and then hold it over the centre-forward's head, just out of reach. A spectacular goalkeeper, he was daring and sometimes even headed shots away !

He was one of the first goalkeepers to elect to throw the ball to a colleague rather than opt for the usual long kick downfield, most used in those days. An excellent shot-stopper, he was a great personality both on and off the field. Although he retired in September 1949, his registration was held by City until May 1955.

Frank Swift was tragically killed in the Munich Air Disaster of 1958 when accompanying Manchester United as a newspaper reporter.

the teams met in the return on 7 April 1948, a crowd of 71,690 witnessed another draw with Linacre scoring for City. Sam Barkas had left the club at the end of the previous season and his replacement was Jock Thomson who led the club to tenth position in their first campaign back in the top flight since the Second World War.

In the opening game of the 1948-49 season, Preston North End's Bobby Langton opened the scoring after just seven seconds but City responded well and goals from Sproston, McDowall and McMorran gave them a 3-2 win. City's England international 'keeper Frank Swift had announced that this would be his last season at Maine Road. His performances throughout the season

Aston Villa	07.91	79	8	23
Manchester City	03.97	7	1	2

BACUZZI David R
Islington	12 October 1940			
Arsenal	05.59	46	0	0
Manchester City	04.64	56	1	0
Reading	09.66	107	0	1

BAKER Gerard A.
U.S.A.	11 April 1938			
Chelsea	06.55	0	0	0
Manchester City	11.60	37	0	14
Ipswich Town	12.63	135	0	58
Coventry City	11.67	27	4	5
Brentford	10.69	6	0	2

BAKER Graham E.
Southampton	3 December 1958			
Southampton	12.76	111 2 22		
Manchester City	08.82	114 3 19		
Southampton	06.87	57	3	8
Aldershot (L)	03.90	7	0	2
Fulham	07.90	8	2	1

BARKAS Samuel
Wardley	29 December 1909			
Bradford City	08.27	202	0	8
Manchester City	04.34	175	0	1

BARLOW Colin J.
Manchester	14 November 1935			
Manchester City	12.56	179	0	78
Oldham Athletic	08.63	6	0	1
Doncaster Rovers	08.64	3	0	0

BARNES Kenneth H.
Birmingham	6 March 1929			
Manchester City	05.50	258	0	18
Wrexham	05.61	132	0	24

BARNES Peter S.
Manchester	10 June 1957			
Manchester City	08.74	108	7	15
West Bromwich Albion	07.79	76	1	23
Leeds United	08.81	31	0	1
Leeds United	08.83	25	2	4
Coventry City	10.84	18	0	2
Manchester United	07.85	19	1	2
Manchester City	01.87	8	0	0
Bolton Wanderers (L)	10.87	2	0	0
Port Vale (L)	12.87	3	0	0
Hull City	03.88	11	0	0
Bolton Wanderers	11.88	2	0	1
Sunderland	02.89	1	0	0

The Blues

Sam Barkas

Born at Tyne Dock, South Shields, Sam Barkas was a brilliant left-back who cost Manchester City £5,000 when signed from Third Division Bradford City in May 1934. He played his first game for the club in a 3-2 defeat at Liverpool at the end of that season, going on to become a first team regular in the four seasons up to the outbreak of the First World War. A most consistent and reliable defender, he always used the ball constructively when playing it out of defence. Sam Barkas was one of four brothers who played football at League level. He was an important member of City's 1936-37 League Championship winning team, figuring in defence alongside Bill Dale and Alex Herd. His only goal for City in 195 League and Cup appearances came against West Bromwich Albion on the opening day of the 1934-35 season. It was his effective goal prevention that endeared him to the Maine Road faithful. He was still fit enough at the age of 38 to captain City to the Second Division Championship in 1946-47. There is no doubt that Sam Barkas would have won more than his five England caps but for the presence of Arsenal's Eddie Hapgood on the international scene. Barkas left Maine Road at the end of that successful 1946-47 campaign to become manager of Workington Town. He later returned to the north-west for a short spell as manager of Wigan Athletic before rejoining the Maine Road club as a scout in 1957. Sam Barkas' achievements are rightly commemorated by a bar named after him in the club's main stand.

helped the Blues to finish in a very creditable seventh position but following his departure, the club were left without a 'keeper as Swift's deputy Alec Thurlow was taken ill with tuberculosis. Thankfully, Swift agreed to come out of retirement and said he would play until a suitable replacement could be found. That replacement was former German paratrooper Bert Trautmann who soon won over the City fans with his courageous displays in a season in which the club finished 21st in the First Division and were relegated.

Jock Thomson was replaced as manager by former City favourite Les McDowall, who had been Wrexham's manager since leaving Maine Road a year earlier. McDowall's aim was simple - to take City back into the First Division.

The club began the 1950-51 season with a 4-2 win at Preston North End and by the end of September were top of the table. The club's captain was Roy Paul, whom McDowall had signed in the close season, and he helped the club remain unbeaten in their first 10 games. City's first defeat was at the hands of Doncaster Rovers who trailed the Maine Road club 3-0 at half-time, but four second-half goals gave the Belle Vue club victory. At the turn of the year, City seemed to lose their way but as the season wore on, got back on track with a 4-1 win at Leeds United and a 6-0 demolition of Barnsley in front of a Maine Road crowd of 42,741. Though the club's last three matches were drawn, City were promoted as runners-up to Preston North End.

Though the fans were hoping for great things on the club's return to the top flight, McDowall's priority had to be survival. After a disappointing start to the 1951-52 season, the City boss signed Ivor Broadis and Don Revie in the hope

BARRETT Colin

Stockport	3 August 1952			
Manchester City	05.70	50	3	0
Nottingham Forest	03.76	64	5	4
Swindon Town	06.80	3	0	0

BARRETT Earl D.

Rochdale	28 April 1967			
Manchester City	04.85	2	1	0
ChesterCity (L)	03.86	12	0	0
Oldham Athletic	11.87	181	2	7
Aston Villa	02.92	118	1	1
Everton	01.95	73	1	0
Sheffield United (L)	01.98	5	0	0
Sheffield Wednesday	02.98	10	5	0

BATTY Michael

Manchester	10 July 1944			
Manchester City	07.61	13	0	0

BEAGRIE Peter S.

Middlesbrough	28November1965			
Middlesbrough	09.83	24	9	2
Sheffield United	08.86	81	3	11
Stoke City	06.88	54	0	7
Everton	11.89	88	26	11
Sunderland (L)	09.91	5	0	1
Manchester City	03.94	46	6	3
Bradford City	07.97	74	3	12
Everton (L)	03.98	4	2	0

BEARDSLEY Peter A.

Newcastle	18 January 1961			
Carlisle United	08.79	93	11	22
Manchester United	09.82	0	0	0
Newcastle United	09.83	146	1	61
Liverpool	07.87	120	11	46
Everton	08.91	81	02	5
Newcastle United	07.93	126	3	47
Bolton Wanderers	08.97	14	3	2
Manchester City (L)	02.98	5	1	0
Fulham	03.98	19	2	4
Hartlepool United	12.98	22	0	2

BECKFORD Darren R.

Manchester	12 May 1967			
Manchester City	08.84	7	4	0
Bury	10.85	12	0	5
Port Vale	03.87	169	9	71
Norwich City	07.91	25	57	

BECKFORD Jason N.

Manchester	14 February 1970			
Manchester City	08.87	8	12	0

The Blues

that the club would soon be challenging Manchester United for the title. Sadly, early in the New Year following three months without a win, City found themselves near the foot of the table. Impressive performances from Bert Trautmann and the fact that there were a number of teams much worse than City meant that the club achieved their season of consolidation by finishing the campaign in 15th place.

After losing their first two games of the 1952-53 season, City met League Champions Manchester United at Maine Road. Goals from Clarke and Broadis gave the Blues a 2-0 lead and though United pulled a goal back towards the end of the game, it wasn't enough and City won their first derby in League football since January 1937. Yet despite this performance, the club struggled in the lower reaches of the First Division, though they did draw with United in the return match at Old Trafford. That season also saw City beat Swindon Town 7-0 in the third round of the FA

Cup with Johnny Hart scoring four of the club's goals, but they were well beaten 5-1 by Luton Town in a replay in the next round. It was Hart who scored City's goal in a 1-0 win at Liverpool a few days after the club's exit from the FA Cup but that victory was one of only a few in the remaining weeks of a season in which the club avoided relegation by just one point.

After a 5-4 win at Sunderland in only the fourth game of the 1953-54 season, City supporters had high hopes that this would not be another season of struggle against relegation. Ivor Broadis left to play for Newcastle United while the club signed Joe Hayes and Billy McAdams in a bid to boost the club's goalscoring rate. McAdams, who joined the club from Distillery, scored on his debut in a 2-1 win over Sunderland and a week later, netted a hat-trick in a 5-2 FA Cup win at Bradford. He endeared himself further to the hearts of the City fans with an equalising goal in the derby match at Old Trafford. However, the remainder of the season was

Eric Westwood

Manchester-born Eric Westwood is one of the few players to have played for both City and United. He started his career as an amateur at Old Trafford before moving across the city to join the Blues in November 1937. It was a year later before he played his first league game for the club as City beat Tottenham Hotspur 2-0. He played in 30 games that season as City ended the campaign in fifth place in Division Two.

During the hostilities, Westwood only managed to appear in 23 wartime games for City but 'guested' for Chelsea, turning out for the Stamford Bridge club in the 1944 War Cup Final.

After helping City win the Second Division Championship in 1946-47, Westwood was ever-present in the next two seasons, his form winning him Football League and England 'B' representative honours. He had scored five goals in 263 League and Cup games when he was given a free-transfer and left Maine Road to play non-league football for Altrincham.

A Concise Post War History of Manchester City

littered with a number of heavy defeats and City had to be content with finishing seven points above the relegation zone in 17th place.

In 1954-55 City manager Les McDowall introduced the Revie Plan in the hope that this would bring the club some long-awaited success. The strategy was named after Don Revie who wore the number nine shirt and depended on a deep-lying centre-forward. Based on the 1953 Hungarian system, it really did confound the opposition. When Manchester United visited Maine Road on 25 September 1954, with the likes of Roger Byrne, Duncan Edwards and Tommy Taylor in their side, they were beaten 3-2. As the season wore on, there was no doubt that the Plan was

Blackburn Rovers (L)	03.91	3	1	0
Port Vale (L)	09.91	4	1	1
Birmingham City	01.92	2	2	1

BEESLEY Paul
Liverpool	21July1965			
Wigan Athletic	09.84	153	2	3
Leyton Orient	10.89	32	0	1
Sheffield United	07.90	162	6	7
Leeds United	08.95	19	3	0
Manchester City	02.97	1030		
Port Vale (L)	12.97	500		
West Bromwich Albion(L)	03.98	8	0	0
Port Vale	08.98	33	2	3

BELL Colin
Hesleden	26 February 1946			
Bury	07.63	82	0	25
Manchester City	03.66	393	1 1	17

BENNETT David A.
Manchester	11July1959			
Manchester City	06.77	43	9	9
Cardiff City	09.81	75	2	18
Coventry City	07.83	157	15	25
Sheffield Wednesday	03.89	20	8	0
Swindon Town	09.90	1	0	0
Shrewsbury Town (L)	11.91	2	0	2

BENSON John H.
Arbroath	23 December 1942			
Manchester City	07.61	44	0	0
Torquay United	06.64	233	7	7
Bournemouth	10.70	35	8	0
Exeter City (L)	03.73	4	0	0
Norwich City	12.73	29	1	1
Bournemouth	01.75	56	1	1

BETTS Barry J.
Barnsley	18 September 1932			
Barnsley	11.50	55	0	0
Stockport County	11.57	112	0	3
Manchester City	06.60	101	0	5
Scunthorpe United	08.64	7	0	0

BIGGINS Wayne
Sheffield	20November1961			
Lincoln City	11.79	8	0	1
Burnley	02.84	78	0	29
Norwich City	10.85	66	13	16
Manchester City	07.88	29	3	9
Stoke City	08.89	120	2	46
Barnsley	10.92	44	3	16
Stoke City	03.94	18	9	6
Luton Town (L)	01.95	6	1	1

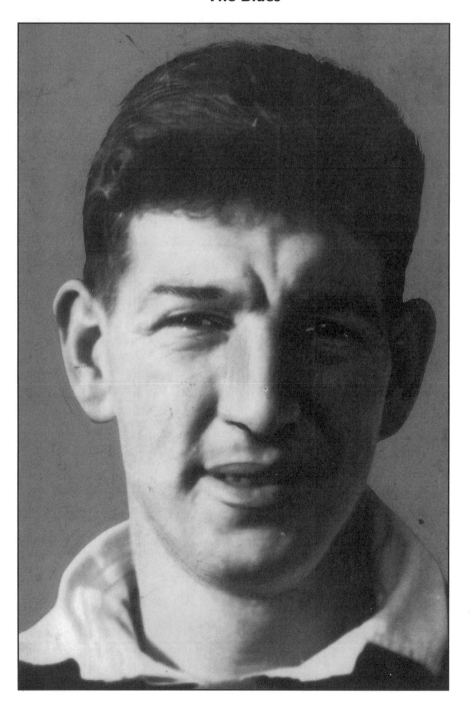

Roy Clarke

Roy Clarke's first taste of international recogntion was as a member of the Welsh Schools Baseball team in 1939. During the Second World War he worked in the coalmines but managed to play football for a local side at the weekends. He later joined Cardiff City, for whom he made 39 appearances and scored 11 goals before joining Manchester City.

Roy Clarke holds the unique record of playing in three different divisions of the Football League in three consecutive league games ! He played his last game for the Bluebirds, who were at the time Third Division Champions, in their penultimate game of the 1946-47 season before he joined the Maine Road club. His debut for the Blues was in their last game of their Second Division promotion-winning season against his home-town club Newport County - a game in which George Smith scored all five goals as City won 5-1. Clarke's next game was at the start of the 1947-48 campaign with City in the top flight. They beat Wolves 4-3 at Molineux with Clarke hitting the winner. He won his first international cap for Wales against England in 1948 and his last eight years later against Northern Ireland, scoring five goals in his 22 games. Roy Clarke was a left-winger with a very powerful shot and scored many vital goals during his Maine Road career. He was instrumental in City getting to Wembley at the end of the 1954-55 campaign. He hit both goals in the 2-0 win at Kenilworth Road as City disposed of Luton Town in the fifth round. He also hit the only goal of the semi-final against Sunderland at Villa Park but unfortunately Newcastle beat them in the final 3-1. The following season, though, he picked up an FA Cup winners' medal as City beat Birmingham 3-1. His best season for City in terms of goals scored was 1956-57 when he netted 11 in his 40 appearances.

In September 1958 he moved on to Stockport County on a free transfer where he played a further 25 league games for the Edgeley Park club.

He returned to Maine Road in 1966 to run the City Social Club. After 22 years he retired on 27 September 1988 with hundreds of friends and colleagues paying tribute to him in a farewell party at Maine Road

The Blues

bringing the best out of the City players. On 29 January 1955, goals from Hayes and Revie helped City beat United for a second time when the two clubs met in the fourth round of the FA Cup, City having beaten Derby County 3-1 in the previous round. The Reds, who were thought by many to be the best side in Britain, soon had a chance to exact revenge, for two weeks after the Cup defeat they entertained City at Old Trafford in the return league match. In one of the most one-sided derby matches of all-time, City won 5-0 with goals from Fagan (2) Hayes (2) and Hart, to equal the margin of the club's biggest win on United's ground, established 29 years earlier. The club continued to play attractive football and ended the campaign in seventh place, just two points behind Wolverhampton Wanderers who were that season's runners-up.

In the FA Cup, City, who of course had beaten United in the fourth round, travelled to Luton in round five, where Roy Clarke scored both goals in a 2-0 win. The Blues had to travel again in round six, this time to St Andrew's where a Johnny Hart goal late in the game was enough to beat Birmingham City. In the semi-final City were paired with Sunderland at Villa Park but had to face the Wearsiders without the services of Johnny Hart, the previous round's goalscorer, after he had broke his leg in a league game at Huddersfield Town a few days earlier. His replacement was Bobby Johnstone who had joined City from Hibernian and it was his pass that set up Joe Hayes' cross from which Roy Clarke headed home the game's only goal. Sadly, Clarke damaged a knee with just a few minutes of the game remaining and though he attempted a comeback, he

Johnny Hart

Johnny Hart was a skilful inside-forward who joined Manchester City from local amateur football. He made his debut for the Blues in a 2-0 home defeat at the hands of Bolton Wanderers in April 1948, though it was 1950-51 before he established himself as a regular member of the club's first team. He was the club's leading scorer in four of the next five seasons, and in January 1953 netted four of the club's goals in a 7-0 FA Cup win over Swindon Town. Towards the end of the 1954-55 season, Hart broke his leg in the match at Huddersfield Town - it was a cruel blow, for not only did it prevent him from playing in the 1955 FA Cup Final but it also signalled the end of his league career. Though he wasn't helped by the presence of Bobby Johnstone, Hart appeared in only 11 more league games over the next six seasons before hanging up his boots. He then spent a decade on the Maine Road staff before becoming manager following the departure of Malcolm Allison. Hart signed Denis Law on a free transfer during his period as manager but after only six months in charge, he was forced to give the position up due to ill health. Hart later returned to Maine Road in the late 1980s to work on the promotional side of the club.

took another knock to the knee in the last league game of the season and had to miss the final against Newcastle United.

FA Cup Final 1955

Manchester City 1 Newcastle United 3

City found themselves a goal dowm after just 45 seconds when Jackie Milburn headed home Len White's corner-kick - it was at the time the fastest goals scored in a Wembley FA Cup Final. City suffered another setback in the 19th minute when Jimmy Meadows damaged his right knee when he turned to tackle Newcastle's winger Bobby Mitchell. He was forced to leave the pitch, reducing the Blues to 10 men.

Oxford United	07.95	3	1	1
Wigan Athletic	11.95	35	16	5

BISHOP Ian W.

Liverpool	29 May 1965			
Everton	05.83	0	1	0
Crewe Alexandra (L)	03.84	4	0	0
Carlisle United	10.84	131	1	14
Bournemouth	07.88	44	0	2
Manchester City	07.89	18	1	2
WestHam United	12.89	240	14	12
Manchester City	03.98	25	6	0

BLACK Andrew

Stirling	23 September 1917			
Manchester City	06.46	139	0	47
Stockport County	08.50	94	0	38

BODAK Peter J.

Birmingham	12August1961			
Coventry City	05.79	30	2	5
Manchester United	08.82	0	0	0
Manchester City	12.82	12	2	1
Crewe Alexandra	12.86	49	4	7
Swansea City	03.88	25	6	4
Walsall (N/C)	08.90	3	1	1

BOND Kevin

West Ham	22 June1 957			
Norwich City	07.74	137	5	12
Manchester City	09.81	108	2	11
Southampton	09.84	139	1	6
Bournemouth	08.88	121	5	4
Exeter City	08.92	19	0	0

BOOK Anthony K.

Bath	4 September 1935			
Plymouth Argyle	08.64	81	0	3
Manchester City	07.66	242	2	4

BOOTH Thomas A.

Manchester	9 November 1949			
Manchester City	08.67	380	2	25
Preston North End	10.81	84	0	2

BOWLES Stanley

Manchester	24 December 1948			
Manchester City	01.67	15	2	2
Bury (L)	07.70	5	0	0
Crewe Alexandra	09.70	51	0	18
Carlisle United	10.71	33	0	12
Queen's Park Rangers	09.72	255	0	70
Nottingham Forest	12.79	19	0	2
Leyton Orient	07.80	46	0	7
Brentford	10.81	80	11	6

The Blues

Bert Trautmann

Arriving in England in April 1945, it was at a Prisoner of War camp at Ashton-in-Makerfield that Bert Trautmann first tried his hand at goalkeeping. He said later that it was his training as a German paratrooper that helped him cushion the ball as he fell. At the end of the Second World War he was released from the Prisoner of War camp and went to work on a farm and began to play for St Helens Town. After some impressive displays he signed for City on 2 November 1949. Seventeen days later he made his first team debut for City against Bolton Wanderers.Replacing the great and popular Frank Swift, Trautmann came in for a great deal of hostility from the Maine Road supporters. This was perhaps not surprising, for war was still fresh in the minds of many people and as an ex-German paratrooper and Prisoner of War, he could hardly have expected the warmest of Lancashire welcomes. Later marrying the City club secretary's daughter, he soon won over the hearts of the Maine Road followers. He was a member of the victorious City side of 1956 that lifted the FA Cup beating Birmingham 3-1 at Wembley. With just 15 minutes remaining, Trautmann dived at the feet of Peter Murphy the Birmingham inside-forward and was caught in the neck by his knee. After receiving lengthy treatment, the 'keeper continued courageously, though he was obviously in great pain. It was only after the match had finished that it was discovered that he had played the closing minutes with a broken neck. He missed the chance to play for his native Germany, being out of the game for the next seven months. Besides his two appearances for City in FA Cup Finals at Wembley, he was voted the 1956 Footballer of the Year. He also had to overcome personal tragedy that same year, when his five-year-old son was killed in a road accident. He retired on 10 May 1964 after playing in 545 games for City. His testimonial match at Maine Road saw a combined City/United team face an international XI before almost 48,000 fans. The game had barely warmed up when United's Maurice Setters in unfamiliar sky blue, killed the ball, turned and with immense power fired a shot past the startled Trautmann and danced for joy at his own goal. 'I've always wanted to score against Bert' he said later 'and tonight was going to be my last chance. I couldn't resist it.'

Trautmann later played non-league football for Wellington Town before becoming general manager of Stockport County and later coaching abroad.

Roy Paul

A native of the Rhondda, Roy Paul was an ex-coalminer who had joined City after making 160 league appearances for Swansea Town, whom he helped win the Third Division (South) Championship in 1948-49. He made his debut for the Maine Road club in a 4-2 win at Preston North End in August 1950 and was a regular in the City side for the next seven seasons. That first campaign saw Paul miss just one game as City won promotion to the the top flight. His performances at half-back won him 33 caps for Wales at full international level though he showed his versatility by also appearing at centre-half for his country. Paul also looked with interest at the situation in Colombia when other British players like Neil Franklin and Charlie Mitten went to Bogota in the hope of a soccer fortune but at the end of the day decided to stay in Britain. After collecting a losers medal in the FA Cup Final of 1955, Paul was back at Wembley twelve months later as captain of the victorious City team that beat Birmingham 3-1.

On leaving City at the end of the following season he became player-manager of non-league Worcester City.

BOWYER Ian
Ellesmere Port	6 June 1951			
Manchester City	08.68	42	81	3
Leyton Orient	06.71	75	3	19
Nottingham Forest	10.73	222	17	49
Sunderland	01.81	15	0	1
Nottingham Forest	01.82	203	3	19
Hereford United	07.87	33	7	1

BOYER Philip J.
Nottingham	25 January 1949			
Derby County	11.66	0	0	0
York City	07.68	108	1	27
Bournemouth	12.70	140	1	46
Norwich City	12.74	115	1	34
Southampton	08.77	138	0	49
Manchester City	11.80	1733		

BRADBURY Lee M.
Isle Of Wight	3 July 1975			
Portsmouth	08.95	41	13	15
Exeter City (L)	12.95	14	0	5
Manchester City	08.97	34	6	10
Crystal Palace	10.98	19	3	4
Birmingham City (L)	03.99	6	1	0

BRADSHAW Carl
Sheffield	2 October 1968			
Sheffield Wednesday	08.86	16	16	4
Barnsley (L)	08.86	6	0	1
Manchester City	09.88	1	4	0
Sheffield United	09.89	59	16	5

BRANAGAN Kenneth F.
Salford	27 July 1930			
Manchester City	11.48	196	0	3
Oldham Athletic	10.60	177	0	5

BRANCH Michael P.
Liverpool	18 October 1978			
Everton	10.95	16	25	3
Manchester City (L)	10.98	4	0	0

BRAND Ralph L.
Edinburgh	18 December 1936			
Manchester City	08.65	20	0	2
Sunderland	08.67	31	0	7

BRANNAN Gerard D.
Prescot	15 January 1972			
Tranmere Rovers	07.90	227	11	20
Manchester City	03.97	38	5	4

The Blues

Sadly the 24-year-old defender had so badly damaged his knee ligaments that he never played again. Now it was a real uphill fight for the Blues who were already without Clarke and Hart. Furthermore, Bert Trautmann was nursing both shoulder and knee injuries when he took to the pitch. Undeterred, City pressed forward and Bobby Johnstone levelled the scores to send the teams in all-square at half-time. In the second half, goals from Mitchell and Hannah gave the Magpies a 3-1 lead which they held to the final whistle. It was the third FA Cup Final victory for Newcastle in a five-year period and was the first one to involve the Blues which had been shown on television. At the club's banquet that evening, City skipper Roy Paul refused to give a speech but when finally persuaded to say a few words, he said 'We'll be back again next year to win it. '

The 1955-56 season proved to be one of the most enjoyable in the club's history though it started on a sour note when Les McDowall suspended Don Revie for 14 days following a major disagreement between the two. Though he was back for the Maine Road derby against United, which City won 1-0 thanks to a Joe Hayes goal, he was dropped for the match at Everton on 19 November 1955. Bobby Johnstone played in the deep lying centre-forward role and City secured a point in a 1-1 draw. Johnstone was replaced midway through the season by Lancashire Cricket Club all-rounder Jack Dyson who scored 13 goals in 25 league games as City ended the campaign in fourth place.

In that season's FA Cup, the third round game against Blackpool at Maine Road had to be abandoned because of thick fog with the Seasiders leading 1-0. In the replay the following week, the teams battled through thick mud and City ran out winners 2-1 with goals from Dyson and Johnstone. A 1-0 win at Southend in the fourth round, courtesy of a Joe Hayes goal, gave City a

Ken Branagan

Full-back Ken Branagan had won Boys' Club international caps for England and Great Britain following a series of consistent displays for North Salford Youth Cup. City had been tracking his progress and eventually in November 1948 he signed professional forms for the Maine Road club. Almost immediately he had to do 18 months National Service in the Army and so his league debut was delayed until December 1950 when he played in the 5-3 defeat of Sheffield United. An ever-present in 1953-54, Branagan was a sound if unspectacular defender who was unlucky to miss both of the club's FA Cup Final appearances in the mid-fifties. Though he only scored three goals in his City career, they were all spectacular efforts, perhaps none more so than the 30-yard drive against Cardiff City in October 1952.

After losing his place in the City side he moved to Oldham Athletic where he teamed up with former City favourites Bobby Johnstone and Bert Lister. Branagan went on to appear in 177 league games for the Latics before leaving the first-class game.

place in round five where they were drawn at home to Liverpool. McDowall brought Don Revie back into the side but he could make little headway as the teams played out a goalless draw on an icy surface. When the teams met at Anfield four days later, the pitch was covered in snow but despite falling behind to an early goal, strikes from Hayes and Dyson gave the Blues a 2-1 win. A crowd of 76,129 watched the sixth round tie between City and Everton at Maine Road, where a goal by Jimmy Harris gave the Merseyside club a 1-0 lead at the interval. City equalised in the 68th minute when Joe Hayes headed home Roy Paul's free-kick. There were just 14 minutes remaining when Bobby Johnstone scored to give

BRENNAN Mark R.
Rossendale   4 October 1965

Ipswich Town	04.83	165	3	19
Middlesbrough	07.88	61	4	6
Manchester City	07.90	25	4	6

BRENNAN Michael
Salford   17 May 1952

Manchester City	12.69	1	3	0
Stockport County	02.72	18	0	3
Rochdale	10.73	35	2	4

BRIGHTWELL David J.
Lutterworth   7 January 1971

Manchester City	04.88	3	1	0
Chester City (L)	03.91	6	0	0
Lincoln City (L)	08.95	5	0	0
Stoke City (L)	09.95	0	1	0
Bradford City	12.95	23	1	0
Blackpool	12.96	1	1	0
Northampton Town	07.97	34	1	1
Carlisle United	07.98	41	0	4

BRIGHTWELL Ian A.
Lutterworth   9 April 1968

Manchester City	05.86	285	36	18
Coventry City	07.98	1	0	0

BRISCOE Lee S.
Pontefract   30 September 1975

Sheffield Wednesday	05.94	36	10	0
Manchester City	02.98	5	0	1

BROADIS Ivor A.
Poplar   18 December 1922

Carlisle United	08.46	91	0	52
Sunderland	02.49	79	0	25
Manchester City	10.51	74	0	10
Newcastle United	10.53	42	0	15
Carlisle United	07.55	159	0	32

BROWN Michael R.
Hartlepool   25 January 1977

Manchester City	09.94	67	22	2
Hartlepool United (L)	03.97	6	0	1

BUCKLEY Gary
Manchester   3 March 1961

Manchester City	04.78	4	2	0
Preston North End	10.81	27	7	2
Bury	03.84	23	8	1

Don Revie

Don Revie began his Football League career with Leicester City but took some time to be appreciated by the Filbert Street crowd. However, his performances in the club's run to the 1949 FA Cup Final in which he scored two goals in the semi-final victory over Portsmouth, won them over. Sadly he missed the Wembley game due to broken blood vessels in his nose.

He was sold to Hull City in November 1949 but lost his form and was switched to wing-half to recover some of his confidence. Following Raich Carter's decision to leave Boothferry Park, Revie asked for a transfer and in October 1951 joined Manchester City for £25,000. He made his debut in a goalless draw at Burnley and over the next six seasons became an integral member of the City side. At Maine Road he was the tactical architect of what became known as the 'Revie Plan'. Revie played as a deep-lying centre-forward who prompted his inside-forwards rather than playing in the traditional style of an out-and-out striker. He masterminded City's 1956 FA Cup Final triumph over Birmingham and won six England caps before a fee of £22,000 took him to Sunderland. After the Wearsiders had been relegated, Revie joined Leeds United and in March 1961 was appointed player-manager. Revie, who was Footballer of the Year in 1955, developed a youth policy at Elland Road and in 1963-64, the Yorkshire club powered their way to the Second Division title. United made an immediate impact in the top flight and in 10 years won two league titles, the FA Cup, the Football League Cup and two Fairs Cups, as well as appearing in numerous other finals. During his reign at Elland Road, Revie was named Manager of the Year in 1969, 1970 and 1972 and was awarded the OBE in January 1970.

In July 1974 he became manager of England but was unable to recapture the club atmosphere at international level. He later left to become coach to the United Arab Emirates, returning to take up a consultancy post at Elland Road in the late 1980s. Struck down by motor neurone disease, he spent his last years confined to a wheelchair, dying in Murrayfield Hospital, Edinburgh in May 1989.

The Blues

City victory by 2-1. The Blues' opponents in the semi-final played at Villa Park were Tottenham Hotspur. In a close fought match, Bobby Johnstone scored the game's only goal when he headed in Roy Clarke's cross to put City into the 1956 FA Cup Final where their opponents were Birmingham City.

Prior to the Cup Final, City's German-born 'keeper Bert Trautmann was awarded the Football Writers' 'Player of the Year' title.

FA Cup Final 1956

Manchester City 3 Birmingham City 1

Don Revie, who for much of the season had been out of favour, replaced Billy Spurdle who was suffering from boils. It was Revie who in the third minute delivered a 40-yard pass to Roy Clarke on the wing. The Welsh international slipped the ball inside to Revie, who in turn laid it in the path of Joe Hayes whose shot beat Gil Merrick in the Birmingham goal to put City 1-0 up. City continued to press forward and Merrick was called into action on a number of occasions before completely against the run of play, Noel Kinsey equalised for Birmingham. In the second-half, City scored twice in the space of two minutes. The first of these goals came in the 65th minute when a move involving Johnstone, Revie and Dyson ended with the latter player

Ken Barnes

As an amateur with non-League Stafford Rangers, his performances attracted the attentions of Birmingham City, West Bromwich Albion and Sheffield Wednesday but it was Manchester City who snapped him up .He played is first game for the club in a 4-2 home win over Derby County in January 1952 though it was his only appearance for the club at league level until the opening game of the 1954-55 season. After that, Barnes was a virtual ever-present in the City side for the next seven seasons, and played in both the 1955 and 1956 FA Cup Finals.

Described by Denis Law as 'the finest uncapped wing-half who ever played English football' Barnes scored a hat-trick of penalties for City in their 6-2 win over Everton at Maine Road in December 1957. For good measure he scored one in the return fixture at Goodison Park.

In May 1961 he joined Wrexham as player-manager and in his first season at the Racecourse Ground, led the Robins to promotion from the Fourth Division, though in 1963-64, they were relegated after two seasons in the higher grade. Mid-way through the following season, Chester beat Wrexham 6-1 and Barnes lost his job to Billy Morris, the man he replaced when he arrived at the Racecourse Ground.

On leaving the Welsh club he moved into non-League football as player-manager of Witton Albion before managing Bangor City. He later returned to Maine Road as trainer-coach before becoming the club's chief scout.

shooting past the advancing Merrick. City's third goal was scored by Bobby Johnstone who beat two defenders before slotting the ball past the Birmingham 'keeper. In doing so, Johnstone became the first player to score in consecutive finals. There were just 14 minutes left when Bert Trautmann in the City goal dived bravely at Murphy's feet. In colliding with the St Andrew's club forward, the injuries he received required lengthy treatment from City's trainer. In spite of the terrific pain he was in, Trautmann persevered until the end of the game and it was only after the final whistle that it was discovered that he had played for almost quarter of an hour with a broken neck !

BURRIDGE John
Workington 3 December 1951

Workington	12.69	27	0	0
Blackpool	04.71	134	0	0
Aston Villa	09.75	65	0	0
Southend United (L)	01.78	6	0	0
Crystal Palace	03.78	88	0	0
Queen's Park Rangers	12.80	39	0	0
Wolverhampton Wands	08.82	74	0	0
Derby County (L)	09.84	6	0	0
Sheffield United	10.84	109	0	0
Southampton	08.87	62	0	0
Newcastle United	10.89	67	0	0
Scarborough	10.93	3	0	0
Lincoln City	12.93	4	0	0
Manchester City	12.94	3	1	0
Notts County	08.95	0	0	0
Darlington	11.95	3	0	0
Grimsby Town	12.95	0	0	0
Northampton Town	01.96	0	0	0
Scarborough	12.96	0	0	0

CAPEL Thomas A.
Manchester 27 June 1922

Manchester City	11.41	9	0	2
Chesterfield	10.47	62	0	27
Birmingham City	06.49	8	0	1
Nottingham Forest	11.49	154	0	69
Coventry City	06.54	36	0	19
Halifax Town	10.55	7	0	1

CARRODUS Frank
Manchester 31 May 1949

Manchester City	11.69	33	9	1
Aston Villa	08.74	150	0	7
Wrexham	12.79	97	0	6
Birmingham City	08.82	7	1	0
Bury	10.83	31	3	1

CARTER Stephen C.
Great Yarmouth 23 April 1953

Manchester City	08.70	4	2	2
Notts County	02.72	172	16	21
Derby County	08.78	32	1	1
Bournemouth	03.82	42	4	1
Torquay United	07.84	16	0	1

CATON Thomas S.
Liverpool 6 October 1962

Manchester City	10.79	164	1	8
Arsenal	12.83	81	0	2
Oxford United	02.87	50	3	3
Charlton Athletic	11.88	56	1	5

The Blues

Roy Paul, who had kept his promise by leading City to victory, walked up the famous Wembley steps to receive the trophy from the Queen.

City began the 1956-57 season without the services of Bert Trautmann who was forced to rest due to his injury in the Cup Final and missed the first few months of the camapign. Also Don Revie was unsettled and after making just 14 league appearances, left Maine Road to join Sunderland for a fee of £24,000. After losing 5-1 at Wolverhampton Wanderers on the opening day of the season, it took the Blues six games to record their first victory. City struggled to win many games and though both George Thompson and John Savage were tried in goal, there is no doubt that a fit Bert Trautmann would have helped the club stem the run of defeats they suffered early in the season. Trautmann returned to the side in mid-December and kept his place until the end of the season as City finished in a disappointing 18th place. He was in the side that met Newcastle United in the third round of the FA Cup as City began their defence of the trophy. After a 1-1 draw at St James' Park, the two teams met at Maine Road four days later. Early in the game, Bob Stokoe put through his own goal to give City the lead. Further goals from Johnstone and Fagan put the Blues 3-0 up after just 25 minutes and this remained the score as the teams went in at half-time. A Tommy Casey

Dave Ewing

Centre-half Dave Ewing joined the Blues from Luncarty Juniors in the summer of 1949, though he had to wait until January 1953 before making his first team debut in a 1-1 draw in the Manchester derby. The following season he was ever-present and went on to miss very few games in the City side over the next nine seasons. Along with Ken Barnes and Roy Paul, Ewing formed one of the best half-back lines in the First Division. His tough, no-nonsense displays in the heart of the City defence helped them reach the FA Cup Final in successive seasons in 1955 and 1956. Dave Ewing holds the unenviable record of the most post-war own goals for City with ten - nine in the league and one in the FA Cup. However, many of his misfortunes came into the 'unlucky' category of own goals - the result of desperate last-ditch clearances in situations where the Blues were totally overrun.

Ewing left Maine Road in the summer of 1962 and joined Crewe Alexandra for whom he made 48 league appearances. He later rejoined City as coach, a position he later held with Sheffield Wednesday, Bradford City and Crystal Palace.

After a spell as manager of Hibernian, Ewing returned to Maine Road for a third time, taking charge of the club's reserve side that won the Central League title for the first time in the club's history in 1977-78.

penalty early in the second-half reduced the arrears and after Tait had added a second, a Bill Curry header in the 85th minute levelled the scores. The match went into extra-time and Bobby Johnstone fired City ahead. The Magpies continued to push forward and Len White scored to bring the scores level at 4-4. The same player then pounced on a pass from Mitchell to score Newcastle's fifth goal. So the Blues lost 5-4, even though they had led 3-0 with barely a third of the game played !

During the summer of 1957, the popular side of Maine Road was roofed and was officially titled the Kippax Street Stand. A lot of the early games in 1957-58 were postponed owing to a flu-

CHADWICK Graham

Oldham	8 April 1942			
Manchester City	03.62	12	0	0
Walsall	08.64	9	0	0
Chester City	07.65	11	1	0

CHANNON Michael R.

Salisbury Plain	28 November 1948			
Southampton	12.65	388	4	157
Manchester City	07.77	71	1	24
Southampton	09.79	119	0	28
Newcastle United	09.82	4	0	1
Bristol Rovers	10.82	4	5	0
Norwich City	12.82	84	4	16
Portsmouth	08.85	34	0	6

CHEETHAM Roy A.

Eccles	2 December 1939			
Manchester City	12.56	127	5	4
Charlton Athletic	10.68	0	0	0
Chester City	12.68	122	2	8

CHRISTIE Trevor

Newcastle	28 February 1959			
Leicester City	12.76	28	3	8
Notts County	06.79	158	29	64
Nottingham Forest	07.84	14	0	5
Derby County	02.85	65	0	22
Manchester City	08.86	9	0	3
Walsall	10.86	91	8	22
Mansfield Town	03.89	88	4	24

CLARKE Jeffrey D.

Pontefract	18 January 1954			
Manchester City	01.72	13	0	0
Sunderland	06.75	178	3	6
Newcastle United	08.82	124	0	4
Brighton & Hove Albion	08.84	4	0	0

CLARKE Roy J.

Newport	1 June 1925			
Cardiff City	12.42	39	0	11
Manchester City	04.47	34	90	73
Stockport County	09.58	25	0	5

CLARKE Wayne

Wolverhampton	28 February 1961			
Wolverhampton Wands	03.78	129	19	30
Birmingham City	08.84	92	0	38
Everton	03.87	46	11	17
Leicester City	07.89	10	1	1
Manchester City	01.90	7	14	2
Shrewsbury (L)	10.90	7	0	6
Stoke City (L)	03.91	9	0	3

A Concise Post War History of Manchester City

Roy Little

Manchester-born full-back Roy Little was playing local football for Greenwood Victoria when spotted by City in the summer of 1949. The tough-tackling defender had to wait until January 1953 before making his first team debut in a 1-0 win at Liverpool. Though he only appeared in three games that season, Little became an established member of the City side early in 1953-54. Cool under pressure and with good distributional skills, he was an important member of the City side, being ever-present in 1955-56. That season, Little won an FA Cup winners' medal after being on the losing side some 12 months earlier. Though he enjoyed going forward, he only scored two goals for the Blues, against Huddersfield Town and Sheffield Wednesday, both in the course of the 1953-54 season.

After nine years at Maine Road he was allowed to leave and join Brighton and Hove Albion where he made 83 league appearances.

On leaving the Goldstone Ground, Little moved to Crystal Palace where he appeared in 38 games before leaving the first-class scene to become player-manager of Southern League Dover.

Wolverhampton Wands (L)03.91   1   0   0

CLAY John H.
Stockport   22 November 1946
Manchester City   05.64   1   1   0

CLEMENTS Kenneth H.
Manchester   9 April 1955
Manchester City   07.75   116   3   0
Oldham Athletic   09.79   204   2   2
Manchester City   03.85   104   2   1
Bury   03.88   66   15   1
Shrewsbury Town   10.90   19   1   0

CLOUGH Nigel H.
Sunderland   19 March 1966
Nottingham Forest   09.84   307   41   01
Liverpool   06.93   29   10   7
Manchester City   01.96   33   5   4
Nottingham Forest (L) 12.96   10   3   1
Sheffield Wednesday (L) 09.97   1   0   0

COLBRIDGE Clive
Hull   27 April 1934
Leeds United   01.52   0   0   0
York City   05.55   37   0   14
Workington   09.57   46   0   8
Crewe Alexandra   10.58   29   0   8
Manchester City   05.59   62   0   12
Wrexham   02.62   108   0   33

COLEMAN Anthony G.
Liverpool   2 May 1945
Tranmere Rovers   10.62   8   0   0
Preston North End   05.64   5   0   1
Doncaster Rovers   11.65   58   0   11
Manchester City   03.67   82   1   12
Sheffield Wednesday   10.69   25   1   2
Blackpool   08.70   17   0   0
Southport   11.73   22   1   1
Stockport County   06.74   28   2   3

CONLON Barry J.
Drogheda   1 October 1978
Manchester City   08.97   1   6   0
Plymouth Argyle (L)   02.98   13   0   2
Southend United   09.98   28   6   7

CONNOR David R.
Wythenshawe   27 October 1945
Manchester City   11.62   130   11   10
Preston North End   01.72   29   0   0

CONWAY James P.
Dublin   10 August 1946

The Blues

Joe Hayes

A relative of the author, Kearsley-born Joe Hayes scored four goals for City in a trial game after arriving at the club with his boots in a brown paper bag ! Within a matter of weeks, he was making his league debut for City at White Hart Lane in a match Spurs won 3-0. Despite suffering from poor eyesight, Joe Hayes soon became a first team regular and though he didn't score for City in his 11 appearances in 1953-54, he more than made up for it in the following nine seasons. In March 1955, Hayes scored his only hat-trick for the club in a 4-2 home win over Bolton Wanderers and the following season netted 27 goals in 49 games including one in the FA Cup Final win over Birmingham City. Hayes' best season in terms of league goals scored was 1957-58 when he netted 25 in 40 games. His prolific marksmanship led to international recognition and he played for England Under-23s, Young England and the FA XI.

Though his total of 152 League and Cup goals make him one of the club's most successful marksmen, it would have been much higher if he hadn't sustained a serious knee injury at Bury in 1964. In July 1965, Hayes left Maine Road to continue his career with Barnsley but after just 26 appearances he returned to the north-west to play for Wigan Athletic and later Lancaster City where he was player-manager.

epidemic but during one week in September, City lost 6-1 at Preston North End and then 9-2 at West Bromwich Albion. In this game at the Hawthorns, City trailed 3-2 with a little over half an hour remaining but after missing a penalty, allowed the Baggies to completely overrun them and record their biggest win of the century. The goals continued to pile up, both for City and their opponents. On 7 December 1957, City beat Everton 6-2, a match in which Ken Barnes scored a hat-trick of penalties and Billy McAdams ended a sequence of scoring in ten consecutive league games by netting two of the club's goals. In the third round of the FA Cup, City drew West Bromwich Albion but were heavily beaten again, this time 5-1. The Blues did eventually get their revenge over Albion, winning 4-1 at Maine Road in the return league meeting between the two clubs. After City had lost 8-4 against Leicester City at Filbert Street, they travelled to Goodison Park for the penultimate game of the season. The home side were two goals up inside the opening two minutes, but by half-time, City had drawn level with Johnny Hart scoring the club's 100th goal of the season. In the second-half, City scored three more goals to win 5-2. The club lost their last game of the season 2-1 at home to Aston Villa, ending the campaign in fifth place and in doing so, became the first side to both score and concede 100 goals or more during a season !

City began the 1958-59 season in fine style, coming back from three goals down to beat Burnley 4-3 at Turf Moor on the opening day of the season. But as the campaign wore on, City struggled near the foot of the First Division and were in danger of losing their place in the top flight. When City played Portsmouth, the Fratton Park club, who

Fulham	05.66	312	4	67
Manchester City	08.76	11	2	1

COOKE Terence J.

Birmingham	5 August 1976			
Manchester United	07.96	1	3	0
Sunderland (L)	01.96	6	0	0
Birmingham City (L)	11.96	1	3	0
Wrexham (L)	10.98	10	0	0
Manchester City	01.99	21	0	7

COOPER Paul D.

Brierley Hill	21 December 1953			
Birmingham City	07.71	17	0	0
Ipswich Town	03.74	447	0	0
Leicester City	06.87	56	0	0
Manchester City	03.89	15	0	0
Stockport County	08.90	22	0	0

CORRIGAN Joseph T.

Manchester	18 November 1948			
Manchester City	01.67	476	0	0
Brighton Hove Albion	09.83	36	0	0
Norwich City (L)	09.84	3	0	0
Stoke City (L)	10.84	9	0	0

COTON Athony P.

Tamworth	19 May 1961			
Birmingham City	10.78	94	0	0
Watford	09.84	233	0	0
Manchester City	07.90	162	1	0
Manchester United	01.96	0	0	0
Sunderland	07.96	10	0	0

CREANEY Gerard T.

Coatbridge	13 April 1970			
Portsmouth	01.94	60	0	32
Manchester City	09.95	81	3	4
Oldham Athletic (L)	03.96	8	1	2
Ipswich Town (L)	10.96	6	0	1
Burnley (L)	09.97	9	1	8
Chesterfield (L)	01.98	3	1	0
Notts County	02.99	13	3	3

CROOKS Lee R.

Wakefield	14 January 1978			
Manchester City	01.95	43111		

CROSS David

Heywood	8 December 1950			
Rochdale	08.69	50	9	21
Norwich City	10.71	83	1	21
Coventry City	11.73	90	1	30
West Bromwich Albion	11.76	38	0	18
West Ham United	12.77	178	1	77

The Blues

had already been relegated, led 2-0 at half-time but four goals in an eight-minute spell midway through the second-half gave the Blues victory 4-3. That result meant that the relegatin spot would go to either Aston Villa or City. Both sides were on 29 points but the Midlands side had a slightly better goal average. Villa's game at fourth placed West Bromwich Albion ended all-square at 1-1 but goals from Hayes Sambrook and McAdams gave City a 3-1 win over Leicester and so condemned the Villa Park outfit to Second Division football the following season.

In the early part of he 1959-60 season, City lost 6-4 at home to Wolverhampton Wanderers but then beat United 3-0 at Maine Road to gain their first League derby victory for four years. During the course of that campaign, 17-year-old Alan Oakes, who was to establish a new club league appearance record, made his debut in a 1-1 home draw against Chelsea and Denis Law was signed from Huddersfield Town for a British record transfer fee of £55,000. The Scotsman scored on his debut in a 4-3 defeat at Leeds United and again in his next match as West Ham United were beaten 2-1 at Maine Road. The Blues ended the season in 16th place, just three points above the relegation zone.

During the 1960 close season, Les McDowall signed Barry Betts and Jackie Plenderleith and three months into the campaign secured the services of Gerry Baker from St Mirren. Despite these new additions, the club endured a mid-season slump and with only a few matches remaining City were level on points with the bottom club. A Denis Law inspired side embarked on an unbeaten run of four games, culminating in a 4-1 home win over Aston Villa which ensured First Division football would be played at Maine Road

in 1961-62. During the course of the 1960-61 season, City played their first-ever Football League Cup match, beating Stockport County 3-0, but lost 2-0 at Second Division Portsmouth in the next round. In the FA Cup it took the Blues three matches to beat fellow First Division club Cardiff City before being drawn away to Luton Town in round four. The Hatters scored twice in the opening 18 minutes of the game but a Denis Law hat-trick gave City a 3-2 lead at half-time. In the second-half, Law scored another three goals and City led 6-2 but with 21 minutes of the game still to play, the referee abandoned the game! Four days later, the game was replayed and though Law scored again for City, Luton won 3-1.

Patsy Fagan

Fionan Fagan or 'Paddy' has he was more commonly known was playing for Transport FC in his native Dublin when his talents where spotted by Hull City. After joining the Tigers, he went on to score two goals in 26 games before signing for City on Christmas Eve 1953. He made his first team debut two days later on Boxing Day as City beat Sheffield United 2-1.

The winger who was equally at home on either flank had his best season in terms of goals scored in 1954-55, finding the net 11 times in 42 games. Though he appeared in that season's FA Cup Final defeat at the hands of Newcastle United, he was missing from the City side the following campaign when they beat Birmingham 3-1 to lift the trophy.

Close control and pin-point crosses were the main features of his play and led to him winning eight full caps for the Republic of Ireland. However in March 1960 after scoring 35 goals in 164 League and Cup games he was transferred to Derby County for a fee of £8,000. With the Rams he scored six goals in 24 games before leaving the Baseball Ground to play non-league football for a number of clubs including Altrincham, Northwich Victoria and Ashton United.

Manchester City	08.82	31	0	12
Oldham Athletic	10.83	18	4	6
West Bromwich Albion	10.84	16	0	2
Bolton Wanderers	06.85	19	1	8
Bury (L)	01.86	12	1	0

CROSSAN John A.

Derry (N.I)	29 November 1938			
Sunderland	10.62	82	0	39
Manchester City	01.65	94	0	24
Middlesbrough	08.67	54	2	7

CUNLIFFE Robert

Manchester	17 May 1945			
Manchester City	08.62	3	0	1
York City	06.65	11	1	2

CUNLIFFE Robert A.

Bryn	27 December 1928			
Manchester City	01.46	44	0	9
Chesterfield	06.56	62	0	19
Southport	07.58	17	0	2

CUNNINGHAM Anthony E.

Jamaica	12 November 1959			
Lincoln City	05.79	111	12	32
Barnsley	09.82	40	21	1
Sheffield Wednesday	11.83	26	2	5
Manchester City	07.84	16	2	1
Newcastle United	02.85	371	0	4
Blackpool	07.87	710	1	7
Bury	07.89	55	31	7
Bolton Wanderers	03.91	9	0	4
Rotherham United	08.91	34	21	7

CURLE Keith

Bristol	14 November 1963			
Bristol Rovers	11.81	21	11	4
Torquay United	11.83	16	0	5
Bristol City	03.84	11	38	1
Reading	10.87	40	0	0
Wimbledon	10.88	91	2	3
Manchester City	08.91	171	0	11
Wolverhampton Wands	08.96	104	1	7

DALEY Stephen J.

Barnsley	15 April 1953			
Wolverhampton Wands	06.71	19	11	38
Manchester City	09.79	47	1	4
Burnley	11.83	20	3	4
Walsall	08.85	28	0	1

DALZIEL Gordon

Motherwell	16 March 1962			
Manchester City	12.83	4	1	0

Bill McAdams

Belfast-born centre-forward who worked as an apprentice heating engineer and played for Bainbridge Town and Glenavon before turning down Burnley after trials. His performances for Irish League club Distillery prompted Manchester City to sign him in December 1953 and he scored on his debut the following month in a 2-1 home win over Sunderland. In only his second game for the Blues, he netted a hat-trick in a 5-2 FA Cup defeat of Bradford City. Despite this impressive start, McAdams found his first few years at Maine Road hampered by injuries, notably a slipped disc and he failed to make the starting line-ups for both the 1955 and 1956 FA Cup Finals.

It was 1957-58 before he became a regular in the City side, scoring 19 goals in 28 games including a hat-trick in a 4-1 home win over West Bromwich Albion. His best season in terms of goals for City was 1959-60 when his total of 21 in 31 games included hat-tricks in the games against Wolves (Home 4-6) Preston North End (Away 5-1) and Newcastle United (Home 3-4). He had scored 65 goals in 134 League and Cup games when in September 1960 he was transferred to Bolton Wanderers.

In his first season with the then Burnden Park club he scored 18 goals in 27 games and continued to play for Northern Ireland, netting a hat-trick against West Germany in a World Cup qualifying game. In December 1961 his former City team-mate Don Revie signed him for Leeds to boost a struggling attack. Although he gained his 15th and final international cap with United, he was soon on the move, joining Brentford in July 1962. He won a Fourth Division Championship medal with the Bees before later playing for Queen's Park Rangers and Barrow where he continued to score goals.

A Concise Post War History of Manchester City

During the summer of 1961, Law left City and signed for Italian giants Torino for £110,000. With the money the club received, McDowall brought Peter Dobing and Bobby Kennedy to Maine Road and they both made their debut in a 3-1 home win over Leicester City. The club made a good start to the 1961-62 campaign, winning six of the opening eight games but by the turn of the year, City were struggling. McDowall introduced 17-year-old Neil Young into the attack and he responded by scoring ten goals in 24 league games. Another youngster brought into the side this season was Glyn Pardoe who was just 15 years 314 days old when he made his first team debut in a 4-1 home defeat by Birmingham City on 11 April 1962. Barry Betts, who had taken over the club captaincy that season, was relieved to see City end the campaign in 12th place especially after the club's dreadful form prior to New Year.

The 1962-63 season started disastrously for City as they were beaten 8-1 by Wolverhampton Wanderers and even the club's goal was scored by the opposition! Another heavy defeat soon followed as West Ham United beat City 6-1 at Maine Road, a match in which Bert Trautmann was sent-off after conceding the fifth goal. The following week, City played United at Old Trafford and went into a two-goal lead inside the first half hour as Peter Dobing from the penalty-spot and a superb strike from Joe Hayes found the target. In the second-half, former City favourite Denis Law, who had joined the Reds in a British record transfer deal, scored twice to level the scores but with almost the last kick of the game, former Third Lanark centre-forward Alex Harley scored the winner for City. Following the worst winter since 1947, many of the club's matches were postponed and

DANIELS Bernard
Salford   24 November 1950

Club				
Manchester United	04.69	0	0	0
Manchester City	04.73	9	4	2
Chester City	07.75	8	1	1
Stockport County	07.76	45	21	7

DAVIDSON David
Govan Hill   28 August 1934

Club				
Manchester City	08.51	1	0	0
Workington	07.58	3	0	0

DAVIDSON Duncan
Elgin   5 July 1954

Club				
Manchester City	09.83	2	4	1

DAVIES Gordon E.
Manchester   4 September 1932

Club				
Manchester City	12.51	13	0	5
Chester City	06.57	22	0	5
Stockport County	08.58	11	0	1

DAVIES Gordon J.
Merthyr Tydfil   8 August 1955

Club				
Fulham	03.78	244	31	14
Chelsea	11.84	11	2	6
Manchester City	10.85	31	0	9
Fulham	10.86	120	27	45
Wrexham	08.91	21	1	4

DAVIES Ian C.
Bristol   29 March 1957

Club				
Norwich City	08.75	29	3	2
Newcastle United	06.79	74	1	3
Manchester City	08.82	7	0	0
Bury (L)	11.82	14	0	0
Brentford (L)	11.83	2	0	0
Cambridge United (L)	02.84	5	0	0
Carlisle United	08.84	4	0	0
Exeter City	12.84	5	0	0
Bristol Rovers	08.85	13	1	1
Swansea City	11.85	11	0	0

DAVIES Wyn R.
Caernarfon   20 March 1942

Club				
Wrexham	04.60	55	0	22
Bolton Wanderers	03.62	155	0	66
Newcastle United	10.66	181	0	40
Manchester City	08.71	4508		
Manchester United	09.72	15	1	4
Blackpool	06.73	34	2	5
Crystal Palace (L)	08.74	3	0	0
Stockport County	08.75	28	2	7
Crewe Alexandra	08.76	50	5	13

The Blues

by the time of the Easter fixtures, the club were next to the bottom of the First Division. The club won two and drew one of their games over the Easter period but then suffered five consecutive defeats to leave them in 21st position with just two games to play. The first of these was the Manchester derby against United at Maine Road. The Reds too were experiencing a difficult season and were only one point ahead of City. In one of the most ill-tempered of derby matches, Alex Harley fired City ahead after nine minutes and though the Scottish striker had the ball in the net again on the half-hour, it was disallowed for offside. City defended resolutely but with just four minutes left, Denis Law was adjudged to have been brought down by Harry Dowd as the

City 'keeper attempted to gather Wagstaffe's underhit back-pass. The referee pointed to the penalty-spot and Albert Quixall sent Dowd the wrong way to level the scores. The game ended all-square at 1-1, leaving City needing to win their last game at West Ham and hope that Birmingham lost theirs. Unfortunately the St Andrew's club won and City were beaten 6-1 at Upton Park, thus ending a stay of 12 seasons in the top flight. The club's relegation signalled the end of Les McDowall's reign as manager and he was replaced for the coming season by his assistant, George Poyser.

City lost the opening game of the 1963-64 season, 2-0 at home to Portsmouth but gradually with experienced signings Derek Kevan and Jimmy Murray among the goals, the

Bill Leivers

Bolsover-born centre-half Bill Leivers began his Football League career with Chesterfield and had made 27 appearances for the Spireites when City paid £10,500 for his services in November 1953. His first season with the club was spent playing Central League football and he had to wait until August 1954 before making his first team debut at Preston North End. It wasn't the best of days for City's young central defender as they crashed to a 5-0 defeat at Deepdale. He made just one more appearance that season before winning a regular first team place midway through the 1955-56 season. After winning an FA Cup winners medal at the end of that campaign, Leivers switched from the heart of the City defence to play right-back, his performances leading to him playing for the FA XI against The Army. Towards the end of his Maine Road career he reverted to right-back and though he suffered numerous injuries, including breaking his nose on five occasions, he went on to appear in 281 League and Cup games before leaving to become player-manager of Doncaster Rovers.

After helping the Belle Vue club to the top of the Fourth Division, he resigned to take charge of Cambridge United. He was manager at the Abbey Stadium when they climbed from the Southern League to the Third Division.

club began to climb up the table. Though in general, results went against them, early in the New Year, the Blues secured a point in a 1-1 draw at Bury with the club's goal being scored by 'keeper Harry Dowd who had broken a finger earlier in the game. A late run which saw the club lose just one of their last nine games allowed City to end the campaign in sixth place. That season's League Cup competition saw City reach the semi-finals after having beaten Carlisle United (Home 2-0) Hull City (Away 3-0) Leeds United (Home 3-1) and Notts County (Away 1-0). In the first leg of the semi-final, City lost 2-0 to Stoke at the Victoria Ground and though Derek Kevan scored in the return leg at Maine Road to give City victory, it wasn't enough to take them through to the final. The club also reached another semi-final that season with City's youngsters going down to Manchester United in the FA Youth Cup.

Inconsistency was certainly the key

DEYNA Kazimierz

Poland	23 October 1947			
Manchester City	11.78	34	4	12

DIBBLE Andrew G.

Cwmbran	8 May 1965			
Cardiff City	08.82	62	0	0
Luton Town	07.84	30	0	0
Sunderland (L)	02.86	12	0	0
Huddersfield Town (L)	03.87	5	0	0
Manchester City	06.88	113	3	0
Middlesbrough (L)	02.91	19	0	0
Bolton Wanderers (L)	09.91	13	0	0
West Bromwich Albion (L)	02.92	9	0	0
Sheffield United	08.97	0	0	0
Luton Town	09.97	1	0	0
Middlesbrough	01.98	2	0	0

DICKOV Paul

Livingston	1 November 1972			
Arsenal	12.90	6	15	3
Luton Town (T)	10.93	8	7	1
Brighton & Hove Alb (L)	03.94	8	0	5
Manchester City	08.96	68	26	24

DOBING Peter A.

Manchester	1 December 1938			
Blackburn Rovers	12.55	179	0	88
Manchester City	07.61	82	0	31
Stoke City	08.63	30	30	80

DOCHERTY Michael

Preston	29 October 1950			
Burnley	11.67	149	4	0
Manchester City	04.76	8	0	0
Sunderland	12.76	72	1	6

DONACHIE William

Glasgow	5 October 1951			
Manchester City	12.68	347	4	2
Norwich City	09.81	11	0	0
Burnley	11.82	60	0	3
Oldham Athletic	07.84	158	11	3

DOWD Harold W.

Manchester	4 July 1938			
Manchester City	07.60	181	0	1
Stoke City (L)	10.69	3	0	0
Oldham Athletic	12.70	121	0	0

DOYLE Michael

Manchester	25 November 1946

The Blues

word for the 1964-65 season as City followed each victory with a defeat. Perhaps the best example being the matches against Leyton Orient. The Blues won the first meeting at Maine Road 6-0 but then went down 4-3 at Brisbane Road a few days later. Midway through the season, the situation reached a crisis point. City, who had been held to a draw at home by Third Division Shrewsbury Town in the FA Cup third round, travelled to Gay Meadow for the replay. They went down 3-1 and a few days later were hosts to Swindon Town. A crowd of just 8,015 turned up for the game,

Maine Road's lowest attendance for a league match. The Wiltshire club won 2-1 and there followed an angry demonstration on the Maine Road forecourt when bricks were thrown at the windows in the ground's Main Stand.

In an effort to appease the suporters, the Board splashed out £40,000 on Sunderland's Northern Ireland international Johnny Crossan and gave a debut to 18-year-old Mike Doyle. With results continued to be disappointing, Poyser resigned his post as manager, though it was to be another few months before a replacement was

Bobby Johnstone

Bobby Johnstone played his early football with Hibernian where his performances alongside the likes of Scottish internationals Gordon Smith, Turnbull, Reilly and Ormond brought him to the attention of a host of top clubs. It was Manchester City who secured his services in March 1955 and after making his debut in a 4-2 home win over Bolton Wanderers, he went on to become an important member of the City side. In January 1956 he scored the first of three hat-tricks for the club in a 4-1 defeat of Portsmouth and at the end of the season in which he had scored 16 goals in 38 games he played in the FA Cup Final defeat by Newcastle United. The following season in which he scored further hat-tricks against Chelsea (Home 5-4) and Cardiff City (Home 4-1) Johnstone became the first man to score in successive Wembley FA Cup Finals when he netted in City's 3-1 win over Birmingham. Whilst with City, Johnstone won four of his total of 17 full caps for Scotland and represented Great Britain against the Rest of Europe.

In September 1959, Johnstone returned to play for Hibernian but within a few months had returned to the north-west to play for Oldham Athletic. The highest Boundary Park crowd for over six years (17,116) saw him score on his debut game against Exeter City in a 5-2 win. He went on to score 42 goals in 143 games for the Latics before hanging up his boots.

The architect of many wonderful wins and the creator of countless magical moments in football - Johnstone can be compared favourably with the likes of Mannion and Doherty as a schemer and ball-artist.

found. The club were unbeaten in their last four games of the season and ended the campaign in 11th place, their lowest-ever league placing at that time.

City's new manager was Joe Mercer, who had played for both Everton and Arsenal before entering management, first with Sheffield United and then Aston Villa. In July 1965 he was joined by Malcolm Allison and so began one of the most successful partnerships in English football, at a club that was in its worst ever state.

The club's first League game under the new management partnership was away to Middlesbrough, Jimmy Murray scoring for City in a 1-1 darw. Over the

Manchester City	05.64	441	7	32
Stoke City	06.78	115	0	5
Bolton Wanderers	01.82	40	0	2
Rochdale	08.83	24	0	1

DYSON Jack
Oldham 8 July 1934
Manchester City	05.52	63	02	5

EDGHILL Richard A.
Oldham 23 September 1974
Manchester City	07.92	123	0	0

EKELUND Ronald M.
Denmark 21 August 1972
Southampton (L)	09.94	15	2	5
Manchester City (L)	12.95	2	2	0

ELLIOTT Andrew
Ashton under Lyne 21 November 1963
Manchester City	11.81	1	0	0
Chester City	09.83	24	8	3

EMPTAGE Albert T.
Grimsby 26 December 1917
Manchester City	02.37	136	0	1
Stockport County	01.51	36	0	1

EWING David
Perth 10 May 1929
Manchester City	06.49	279	0	1
Crewe Alexandra	07.62	48	0	0

FAGAN Fionan (Paddy)
Dublin 7 June 1930
Hull City	03.51	26	0	2
Manchester City	12.53	153	0	34
Derby County	03.60	24	0	6

FAGAN Joseph F.
Liverpool 12 March 1921
Manchester City	10.38	148	0	2
Bradford Park Avenue	08.53	3	0	0

FASHANU Justin S.
Hackney 19 February 1961
Norwich City	12.78	84	6	35
Nottingham Forest	08.81	31	1	3
Southampton (L)	08.82	9	0	3
Notts County	12.82	63	1	2
Brighton & Hove Albion	06.85	16	0	2
Manchester City	10.89	0	2	0
West Ham United	11.89	2	0	0
Leyton Orient	03.90	3	2	0
Torquay United	12.91	21	0	10

The Blues

Cliff Sear

Left-back Cliff Sear was working as a miner at Bershaw Colliery when he was first on City's books as an amateur before being offered professional terms in January 1957. After some impressive performances in the club's Central League side, he was given his first team debut at Birmingham City in April of that year in a match the Blues drew 3-3. Early the following season he settled into the City side and over the next few difficult seasons, Sear was one of the club's most consistent performers. After captaining the Welsh Under-23 side, he won his only full cap for his country when he played against England in 1962.

Sear went on to appear in 279 League and Cup games for City before leaving Maine Road in April 1968 to join Chester City. He appeared in a further 51 league games for the then Sealand Road club before becoming the club's youth team coach working alongside his former City colleague Alan Oakes who had become Chester's manager.

FAULKNER Roy V.

Manchester	28 June 1935			
Manchester City	12.52	7	0	4
Walsall	03.58	102	0	46

FENTON Nicholas L.

Preston	23 November 1979			
Manchester City	11.96	3	0	0

FIDLER Dennis J.

Stockport	22 June 1938			
Manchester City	01.57	5	0	1
Port Vale	06.60	38	0	12
Grimsby Town	04.63	142	1	40
Darlington	10.66	32	2	3

FLEET Stephen

Salford	2 July 1937			
Manchester City	02.55	5	0	0
Wrexham	06.63	79	0	0
Stockport County	01.66	36	0	0

FLEMING Gary J.

Derry (NI)	17 February 1967			
Nottingham Forest	11.84	71	3	0
Manchester City	08.89	13	1	0
Notts County (L)	03.90	3	0	0
Barnsley	03.90	236	3	0

FLITCROFT Garry W.

Bolton	6 November 1972			
Manchester City	07.91	109	6	13
Bury (L)	03.92	12	0	0
Blackburn Rovers	03.96	66	6	5

FOSTER John

Manchester	19 September 1973			
Manchester City	07.92	17	2	0
Carlisle United	03.98	7	0	0
Bury	07.98	6	1	0

FRANCIS Trevor

Plymouth	19 April 1954			
Birmingham City	05.71	278	21	18
Nottingham Forest	02.79	69	1	28
Manchester City	09.81	26	0	12
Queen's Park Rangers	03.88	30	2	12
Sheffield Wednesday	02.91	28	42	5

FRONTZECK Michael

Germany	26 March 1964			
Manchester City	01.96	19	4	0

The Blues

next couple of weeks, the Blues did the double over Wolves, a side that had been relegated the previous season, winning 2-1 at home and 4-2 at Molineux. Ralph Brand from Rangers had been Mercer's first signing but unfortunately he never displayed his true form at Maine Road. His second signing was Mike Summerbee who joined the club from Swindon Town for a fee of £35,000 and he was joined in the early part of the season by Everton's reserve centre-half, George Heslop. Undefeated in their opening seven games, City were top of the Second Division by the end of Otcober. By Christmas, City had slipped to third place but on New Year's Day 1966, entertained league leaders Huddersfield Town. The season's highest league attendance of 47,171 watched City win 2-0. As well as riding high in the league, the club made progress in the FA Cup. They knocked out Blackpool (Home 3-1 after a 1-1 draw) Grimsby Town (Home 2-0) and Leicester City (Away 1-0 after a 2-2 draw) before meeting Everton in the quarter-final. A crowd of 63,034 witnessed the Maine Road encounter but the game ended goalless with very few chances falling to either side. The replay at Goodison Park produced the same result and so the tie necessitated a third meeting which the Mersey-siders won 2-0 at neutral Molineux.

Back in the League, City were still in the promotion pack but the Cup run had stretched the club's playing resources to the full and new faces were required.

City signed Colin Bell from Bury for £45,000 and he scored on his debut in a 2-1 win over Derby County. On 4 May 1966, Bell scored the only goal of the game against Rotherham United which secured promotion for the club and then just over a week later, they beat Charlton Athletic at The Valley 3-2 to win the Second Division Championship.

The top of the Second Division table

Colin Barlow

Colin Barlow joined City from Tarporley Boys' Club and after impressing in the club's Central League side, made his first team debut in the opening game of the 1957-58 season, scoring in a 3-2 win at Chelsea. He held his place in the side for the rest of the season, scoring 17 goals in 39 games as the Blues finished fifth in Division One. He repeated the feat the following season, his 17 goals making him the club's leading scorer and included hat-tricks in the wins over Tottenham Hotspur (Home 5-1) and West Ham United (Home 3-1). Forming a prolific goalscoring partnership with Billy McAdams, he had his best season in terms of goals scored in 1959-60, netting 19 in 39 outings, including scoring in six successive games. Barlow went on to score 80 goals in 189 League and Cup games for City before leaving Maine Road in the summer of 1963 to join Oldham Athletic.

Hampered by injuries at Boundary Park, he spent just one season with the Latics before signing for Doncaster Rovers where he ended his league career.

A Concise Post War History of Manchester City

in 1965-66 looked like this:

	P.	W.	D.	L.	F.	A.	Pts
Manchester City	42	22	15	5	76	44	59
Southampton	42	22	10	10	85	56	54
Coventry City	42	20	13	9	73	53	53

During the close season, City signed 31-year-old full-back Tony Book from Malcolm Allison's old club, Plymouth Argyle. He made an im-pressive debut in the club's opening game of the 1966-67 season as City drew 1-1 at Southampton. The first game at Maine Road saw the Blues take on the reigning League Champions Liverpool in front of a 50,320 crowd. Goals from Bell and Murray gave City a surprise 2-1 victory. In the return at Anfield the following

FROST Ronald A.
Stockport	16 January 1947			
Manchester City	05.64	2	0	1

FUTCHER Paul
Chester	25 September 1956			
Chester City	01.74	20	0	0
Luton Town	06.74	131	0	1
Manchester City	06.78	36	1	0
Oldham Athletic	08.80	98	0	1
Derby County	01.83	35	0	0
Barnsley	03.84	229	1	0
Halifax Town	07.90	15	0	0
Grimsby Town	01.91	51	0	0

FUTCHER Ronald
Chester	25 September 1956			
Chester City	01.74	4	0	0
Luton Town	06.74	116	4	40
Manchester City	08.78	10	7	7
Barnsley	12.84	18	1	6
Oldham Athletic	07.85	65	0	30
Bradford City	03.87	35	7	18
Port Vale	08.88	46	6	20
Burnley	11.89	52	5	25
Crewe Alexandra	07.91	18	3	4

GAUDINO Maurico
Germany	12 December 1966			
Manchester City	12.94	17	3	0

GAYLE Brian W.
Kingston	6 March 1965			
Wimbledon	10.84	76	7	3
Manchester City	07.88	55	0	3
Ipswich Town	01.90	58	0	4
Sheffield United	09.91	115	2	9
Exeter City	08.96	10	0	0
Rotherham United	10.96	19	1	0
Bristol Rovers	03.97	23	0	0
Shrewsbury Town	12.97	66	1	0

GIDMAN John
Liverpool	10 January 1954			
Aston Villa	08.71	196	1	9
Everton	10.79	64	0	2
Manchester United	08.81	94	1	4
Manchester City	10.86	52	1	1
Stoke City	08.88	7	3	0
Darlington	02.89	13	0	1

GILL Raymond
Manchester	8 December 1924			
Manchester City	09.47	8	0	0

Alan Oakes

Alan Oakes left school at 15 after representing Mid-Cheshire boys and immediately joined Manchester City. He had always played inside-forward in school football but had a number of games at wing-half for the county and it was this position he adopted when he joined City. He made his league debut against Chelsea in November 1959 as a stand-in for the injured Ken Barnes. In his debut season he had to help City fight against relegation which was only avoided when Colin Barlow's goal secured victory over Preston North End. It was towards the end of the following season when Ken Barnes left to join Wrexham that Oakes established himself in the City side. His early years at Maine Road in the first half of the 1960s were spent in a poor City side. However, Oakes held on and was rewarded with plenty of honours in the remainder of his career with City. He won a Second Division Championship medal, followed by a League Championship medal, two League Cup winners' medals, an FA Cup winners' medal and a European Cup Winners' Cup medal. He didn't manage to acquire a full England cap but he did play for the Football League against the Scottish League at Hampden Park in March 1969. Over the two seasons prior to this he had been chosen for the full England squad on three occasions but still awaited that elusive first cap. There have certainly been more flamboyant footballers than Alan Oakes who have won England caps but certainly not as talented. He was a player who made great surging runs from midfield, Young and Coleman in particular benefiting.

Despite playing at wing-half, he was always fortunate enough to score a number of goals for City. Against Athletico Bilbao in the second leg of the European Cup Winners' Cup match at Maine Road, after the first match had been drawn 3-3, he let fly from fully 30 yards as the Spanish defence backed off and the ball rocketed into the net. Another Oakes special came against Swindon Town when Mike Summerbee (not yet with City) threw the ball to a surprised Oakes, he killed it, swung round at it terrifically hard from 40 yards with his left foot to score.

He was rewarded with a testimonial against Manchester United in 1972 and to mark his 500th appearance he was presented with a silver salver before the game against Stoke City in November 1974.

In July 1976, having helped City to yet another success at Wembley, he signed for Chester for £15,000, later becoming their player-manager. His part in the history of Manchester City Football Club cannot be over-estimated. He played in 669 games for City - more than any other player.

The Blues

44

Denis Law

Denis Law was one of the great strikers and characters in the modern game, yet when he arrived at Huddersfield Town from Aberdeen in 1956, he was a thin bespectacled 16-year-old who looked nothing like a footballer. Law signed professional forms for Huddersfield in February 1957. The following year he became Scotland's youngest player in modern times when he made his debut against Wales aged 18 years 236 days. He stayed with the Yorkshire club until March 1960 when Manchester City paid Huddersfield Town £55,000 for his services. It was a League record fee, surpassing the previous British transfer record by £10,000. Making his City debut at Elland Road, Law scored one of the Blues' goals in a 4-3 defeat by Leeds United. On 28 January 1966, Denis Law produced a display of a lifetime to score six goals in a fourth round FA Cup tie, onl;y for the referee to abandon the game with 21 minutes to play. Luton Town were the opponents at Kenilworth Road, racing into a two-goal lead within the first 18 minutes. However, before half-time, Law had completed his hat-trick and within 24 minutes of the second-half, he had collected a second hat-trick ! His six goals had come in the space of 48 minutes but conditions were worsening and the referee ended the game. A few days later when it was replayed, City lost 3-1 with that man Law scoring again.

On 13 July 1961, Italian giants Torino paid £100,000 for Law's skills. It was the first time that a British club had been involved in a six-figure transfer. Twelve months later he joined Manchester United when they became the first British club to pay over £100,000 for a player. He scored on his United debut in August 1962 as the Reds drew 2-2 at West Bromwich Albion. On 3 November 1962 he scored four goals for United against Ipswich Town and then four days later scored a further four goals for Scotland against Norway. A year earlier, he had scored four goals for Scotland against Northern Ireland. Law rounded off a superb first season by scoring at Wembley as United beat Leicester City 3-1 to win the FA Cup. Denis Law claims the existing record for the most hat-tricks to have been scored in European Cup competitions by anyone for a Football League club. Soon his goals in between lengthy bouts of suspension as he rebelled against the increasingly harsh treatment he was receiving were inspiring United to two League Championships but unfortunately he had to watch United's 4-1 win over Benfica in the 1968 European Cup Final from his hospital bed after a knee operation.

Though his disciplinary record stopped him from being voted Footballer of the Year, the English soccer writers' counterparts on the continent voted him European Footballer of the Year in 1964. He never reached the same heights again but he did enjoy an Indian summer with Manchester City as he returned to Maine Road in July 1973. He made another Wembley appearance with City and at the close of his international career, at last enjoyed a trip to the World Cup in Germany in 1974 by which time he was 34.

Ironically his last league goal was a cheeky back-heel consigning United to the Second Division !

The Blues

week, City, who had just beaten Sunderland 1-0, went down 3-2. The club then failed to win any of the next four games before visiting Old Trafford for the Manchester derby. United won 1-0 with former Blue, Denis Law scoring the game's only goal. It was around this time that the club brought in England athlete Derek Ibbotson in an attempt to make City the fittest club side in Europe. The move was a good one and in the months leading up to the turn of the year, results improved. However, by the time of the Maine Road derby, City had slipped to fourth from bottom of the First Division and were in desperate need of two points. It wasn't to be, for in a game played in atrocious conditions, the Blues had to

settle for a point in a 1-1 draw. Eventually the club began to edge away from the danger zone and ended their first season back in the top flight in 15th place.

That season's FA Cup competition saw City reach the quarter-final after wins over Leicester City (Home 2-1) Cardiff City (Home 3-1 after a 1-1 draw) and Ipswich Town (Away 3-0 after a 1-1 draw). The sixth round saw the Blues travel to Elland Road to play Don Revie's Leeds United. The Maine Road club were desperately unlucky to lose 1-0 with the Yorkshire club's goal scored by Jack Charlton being allowed to stand despite the England centre-half impeding Harry Dowd the City 'keeper.

After gaining just one point from the

Bobby Kennedy

Motherwell-born full-back and wing-half Bobby Kennedy overcame a very serious illness which kept him out of the game for almost a year. He went on to appear in two Scottish Cup Finals for Kilmarnock and helped the Rugby Park club to finish the 1959-60 and 1960-61 seasons as runners-up in the Scottish League First Division.

In the summer of 1961, City paid 45,000 to bring Kennedy to Maine Road, at the time a record for a wing-half. He scored on his debut in a 3-1 home win over Leicester City and was ever-present at the end of his first season with the Blues. In eight seasons with the club, Kennedy missed very few games and though the club were not having the best of times during his early years with them, he was the club's first-choice left-back, having been converted earlier in the season, when they won promotion to the First Division in 1965-66.

In March 1968 he left Maine Road to become player-manager of Grimsby Town where after making 84 league appearances he resigned. He then managed Bradford City's youth team before having a brief spell with League of Ireland club Drogheda.

He then took over as 'honorary' manager of Bradford Park Avenue before becoming full-time boss of Bradford City. He led the Bantams to promotion in 1976-77 but in January 1978 with the club struggling at the wrong end of Division Three he was controversially sacked.

A Concise Post War History of Manchester City

opening three games of the 1967-68 season, City embarked on an unbeaten five-match run that took them towards the top of the table. Their next match was the Maine Road derby in which former Stockport County 'keeper Ken Mulhearn made his debut. Despite taking the lead with an early goal by Colin Bell, the Blues lost 2-1 with Bobby Charlton netting both the Reds' goals. On 9 October 1967, City paid £60,000 for the services of Bolton's Francis Lee and he made his debut against Wolverhampton Wanderers five days later. From then until Boxing Day, the Blues were unbeaten in 11 League games.

During this period, City played Spurs on a Maine Road pitch that was covered with snow. Jimmy Greaves opened the

Chester City	06.51	406	0	3

GLEGHORN Nigel W.
Seaham	12 August 1962			
Ipswich Town	08.85	54	12	11
Manchester City	08.88	27	7	7
Birmingham City	09.89	142	03	3
Stoke City	10.92	162	4	26
Burnley	07.96	33	1	4
Brentford (L)	11.97	11	0	1
Northampton Town (L)	02.98	3	5	1

GLENNON Christopher D.
Manchester	29 October 1949			
Manchester City	11.67	3	1	0
Tranmere Rovers	01.71	2	0	0

GOATER Shaun L.
Hamilton, Bermuda	25 February 1970			
Rotherham United	10.89	169	40	70
Notts County (L)	11.93	1	0	0
Bristol City	07.96	67	8	40
Manchester City	03.98	48	2	20

GODWIN Verdi
Blackpool	11 February 1926			
Blackburn Rovers	03.46	27	0	6
Manchester City	06.48	8	0	3
Stoke City	06.49	22	0	2
Mansfield Town	01.50	31	0	9
Grimsby Town	01.52	1	0	0
Brentford	03.52	7	0	0
Southport	07.54	17	0	2
Barrow	08.55	16	0	3
Tranmere Rovers	08.56	14	0	2

GOLAC Ivan
Yugoslavia	15 June 1950			
Southampton	11.78	143	1	4
Bournemouth (L)	11.82	9	0	0
Manchester City (L)	03.83	2	0	0
Southampton	03.84	24	0	0
Portsmouth (L)	01.85	8	0	0

GOMERSALL Victor
Manchester	17 June 1947			
Manchester City	07.60	39	0	0
Swansea City	08.66	179	1	6

GOW Gerald
Glasgow	29 May 1952			
Bristol City	06.69	367	7	48
Manchester City	10.80	26	0	5
Rotherham United	01.82	58	0	4
Burnley	08.83	8	1	0

Neil Young

One of Manchester City's first-ever apprentice professionals, Neil Young signed for City in the close season of 1960. He made his league debut in November 1961 at Aston Villa and though the Blues lost, he had the satisfaction of setting up Peter Dobing for the City goal. His first goal for the club came in his fifth game in a 3-0 win over Ipswich Town. In these early days he was being switched around the forward line but when Mercer and Allison moved him permanently to the No.10 spot he flourished. They gave him a free-roving commission and he repaid their faith in him by scoring 17 League and Cup goals including a hat-trick in a 5-0 defeat of Leyton Orient, to end the 1965-66 season as the club's leading scorer. He top-scored again in City's League Championship winning season of 1967-68 with 22 goals and crowned a great season by scoring twice in the club's 4-3 win at Newcastle United.

It was Neil Young's splendid left-foot shot that won the Blues the FA Cup in 1969. The following year he scored one of City's two goals in Vienna which brought victory over Gornik Zabrze in the European Cup Winners' Cup. In January 1972 Young moved to Preston North End for £48,000 and later had a short spell with Rochdale before retiring.

A player who always seemed to have something to spare, he is best remembered for his excellent ball control and shooting power which helped to bring so much success to Maine Road.

GRATRIX Roy
Salford — 9 February 1932

Club				
Blackpool	03.53	400	0	0
Manchester City	09.64	15	0	0

GRAY Matthew
Renfrew — 11 July 1936

Manchester City	03.63	87	4	21

GREALISH Anthony P.
Paddington — 21 September 1956

Leyton Orient	07.74	169	2	10
Luton Town	08.79	78	0	2
Brighton & Hove Albion	07.81	95	5	6
WestBromwich Albion	03.84	55	10	5
Manchester City	10.86	11	0	0
Rotherham United	08.87	105	5	7
Walsall	08.90	32	4	1

GREENACRE Christopher M.
Halifax — 23 December 1977

Manchester City	07.95	3	5	1
Cardiff City (L)	08.97	11	0	2
Blackpool (L)	03.98	2	2	0
Scarborough (L)	12.98	10	2	2

GREENWOOD John E.
Manchester — 22 January 1921

Manchester City	09.46	1	0	0
Exeter City	06.49	31	0	2
Aldershot	03.51	12	0	0
Halifax Town	11.51	0	0	0

GRIFFITHS Carl B.
Welshpool — 16 July 1971

Shrewsbury Town	09.88	110	33	54
Manchester City	10.93	11	7	4
Portsmouth	08.95	2	12	2
Peterborough United	03.96	6	10	2
Leyton Orient (L)	10.96	5	0	3
Leyton Orient	03.97	60	5	29
Wrexham (L)	01.99	4	0	3
Port Vale	03.99	3	0	1

GROENENDIJK Alphonse
Netherlands — 17 May 1964

Manchester City	08.93	9	0	0

GUNNING James M.
Helensburgh — 25 June 1929

Manchester City	11.50	13	0	0
Barrow	07.54	10	0	1

The Blues

scoring for the White Hart Lane club as early as the seventh minute but with snow continuing to fall, Colin Bell levelled the scores. In the second-half, City ran the London club ragged and goals from Summerbee, Coleman and Young gave the Blues a 4-1 win. It was a classic game of football and one that is still talked about today by supporters of that generation. At the turn of the year, City were in third position behind Liverpool and Manchester United.

In the FA Cup, the Blues beat Reading 7-0 at Elm Park but were then knocked out in the fourth round by Leicester City. The Foxes won 4-3 at Filbert Street after the first game at Maine Road had been goalless.

Now able to concentrate solely on the League, City went to the top of the table for the first time after beating Fulham 5-1. There then followed a 2-0 defeat at Leeds United before the Blues visited Old Trafford for the Manchester derby. A crowd of 63,004 saw George Best give United the lead after just 38 seconds before Colin Bell levelled the scores after quarter-of-an-hour. Twelve minutes into the second-half and George Heslop scored his first league goal for the club before Francis Lee sealed a great win for City with a penalty awarded for a foul on Colin Bell by Burns. Bell, who had been excellent throughout the game, was carried off on a stretcher with an injured knee and forced to miss the next four games. Two of those games saw City lose 1-0 at

Glyn Pardoe

The cousin of Alan Oakes, Glyn Pardoe was only 15 years 314 days old when he made his league debut for City against Birmingham on 11 April 1962. He kept his place for a further three games before being rested, but it was obvious that the youngster had great potential.

What was not yet apparent was his best position. As a schoolboy he had played centre-half for his school team but was converted to centre-forward by the England Boys' manager and against Wales in 1960-61, scored four goals. For City in 1963-4 he played in a variety of positions and it wasn't until Mercer and Allison arrived that he turned out at left-back, a position he was to keep for some years to come.

In 1967-68 he won four England Under-23 caps as City won the League Championship for the second time in their history. He even got on to the score sheet in the 1970 League Cup Final, hitting home the winning goal in extra-time as City beat West Bromwich Albion 2-1. Then on 12 December 1970, he broke a leg in the Manchester derby game. Not only did Glyn almost lose his leg, which had five fractures and a trapped main artery but his life was also in danger and it was the speed and skill of the surgeons that saved him.

Apart from 1973-74 when he made 31 league appearances, he never regained a regular place in the City side. He joined the club's coaching staff, working with reserves and juniors for ten years. A loyal servant of the club, he not only won many honours but also did a valuable job in bringing on the younger players.

both Leicester and Chelsea. With just four games to play, the Blues were in third place, four points behind League leaders Manchester United, but with a game in hand. After beating Sheffield Wednesday 1-0, goals from Book and Coleman gave the club a 2-0 victory over Everton. City were now top of the table with just two league matches remaining. On 4 May, they moved nearer the elusive title with a 3-1 victory at Tottenham Hotspur. Now there was just one game left, against Newcastle United at St James' Park but the Reds were still in the driving seat, as they had a better goal average and were at home to lowly Sunderland for their last game.

On the day of the game, some 19,000

HADDINGTON Raymond W.
Scarborough	18 November 1923			
Bradford City	09.46	0	0	0
Oldham Athletic	08.47	117	0	63
Manchester City	11.50	6	0	4
Stockport County	12.51	11	0	4
Bournemouth	07.52	2	0	0
Rochdale	10.52	38	0	12
Halifax Town	11.53	8	0	0

HAMMOND Geoffrey
Sudbury	24 March 1950			
Ipswich Town	07.68	52	3	2
Manchester City	09.74	33	1	2
Charlton Athletic	07.76	15	1	0

HANNAH George
Liverpool	11 December 1928			
Newcastle United	09.49	167	0	41
Lincoln City	09.57	38	0	4
Manchester City	09.58	114	0	15
Notts County	07.64	25	0	1
Bradford City	10.65	29	1	2

HANNAWAY Jack
Bootle	22 October 1927			
Manchester City	04.50	64	0	0
Gillingham	06.57	126	0	4
Southport	06.60	73	0	2

HAREIDE Age F.
Norway	23 September 1953			
Manchester City	10.81	17	7	0
Norwich City	11.82	38	2	1

HARLEY Alexander
Glasgow	20 April 1936			
Manchester City	08.62	40	0	23
Birmingham City	08.63	28	0	9

HARPER Alan
Liverpool	1 November 1960			
Liverpool	04.78	0	0	0
Everton	06.83	103	24	4
Sheffield Wednesday	07.88	32	3	0
Manchester City	12.89	46	4	1
Everton	08.91	4560		
Luton Town	09.83	40	1	1
Burnley	08.94	30	1	0
Cardiff City (L)	11.95	5	0	0

HART John P.
Golborne	8 June 1928			
Manchester City	06.45	169	0	67

The Blues

Mike Doyle

Mike Doyle was a very determined player in whatever position he was given. He made his first team debut for Manchester City as a centre-forward against Cardiff City in March 1965 after a series of impressive displays for the Youth and Central League sides. It was his influence during the 1965-66 season that went a long way in helping City get out of the Second Division. Certainly not a prolific goalscorer, when he did score they were usually important goals. He scored six goals in a four-match spell over the Christmas period that season to help consolidate City's position at the top of the division. He was also instrumental in City topping the First Division in 1967-68. It was during this season that he played his first representative game, playing for England Under-23s against Hungary and for Young England against an England XI. There followed appearances for the Football League, the first in 1972 against the Scottish League.

Doyle seemed to save his goals for the European competitions or for the domestic trophy finals. He scored the equalising goal at Wembley in the 1970 League Cup Final after West Brom had gone a goal up and in April 1970 he scored one of the goals in the European Cup Winners' Cup semi-final second leg against Schalke 04, City winning 5-1 after losing by the only goal in Germany. He also scored against Gornik Zabrze in the 1970-71 Cup Winners' Cup campaign. Doyle scored to make it 2-2 on aggregate and force a third match in Copenhagen which City won 3-1. Unfortunately City lost to Chelsea in the two-legged semi-final with Doyle missing both matches due to injury.

Mike Doyle was one of City's finest players under Mercer and Al;lison and later Tony Book, winning two League Cup winners' medals, an FA Cup winners' medal and a European Cup Winners' Cup medal.

After Rodney Marsh left Maine Road in 1975, Doyle was made club captain and a year later made the first of his five full international appearances for England against Wales.

After struggling to get back into the City side after injury, he was transferred to Stoke City for £50,000 in June 1978. After playing in over 100 games for the Potters he joined Bolton, later playing for Rochdale before hanging up his boots.

HARTFORD Asa R.

Clydebank	24 October 1950			
West Bromwich Albion	11.67	206	8	18
Manchester City	08.74	184	1	22
Nottingham Forest	07.79	3	0	0
Everton	08.79	81	0	6
Manchester City	10.81	75	0	7
Norwich City	10.84	28	0	2
Bolton Wanderers	07.85	81	0	8
Stockport County	06.87	42	3	0
Oldham Athletic	03.89	3	4	0
Shrewsbury Town	08.89	22	3	0

HAYDOCK William E.

Salford	19 January 1937			
Manchester City	03.59	3	0	1
Crewe Alexander	03.61	142	0	30
Grimsby Town	11.64	21	0	4
Stockport County	08.65	257	4	4
Southport	11.71	7	0	0

HAYES Joseph

Kearsley	20 January 1936			
Manchester City	08.53	331	0	142
Barnsley	07.65	26	0	2

HEALEY Ronald

Manchester	30 August 1952			
Manchester City	10.69	30	0	0
Coventry City (L)	12.71	3	0	0
Preston North End (L)	12.73	6	0	0
Cardiff City	03.74	216	0	0

HEANEY Neil A.

Middlesbrough	3 November 1971			
Arsenal	11.89	4	3	0
Hartlepool United (L)	01.91	2	1	0
Cambridge United (L)	01.92	9	4	2
Southampton	03.94	42	19	5
Manchester City	11.96	13	5	1
Charlton Athletic (L)	03.98	4	2	0
Bristol City (L)	03.99	2	1	0

HEATH Adrian P.

Stoke	11 January 1961			
Stoke City	01.79	94	1	16
Everton	01.82	206	20	71
Aston Villa	08.89	8	1	0
Manchester City	02.90	58	17	3
Stoke City	03.92	5	1	0
Burnley	08.92	8	1	0
Sheffield United	12.95	0	4	0
Burnley	03.96	1	4	0

Mike Summerbee

Mike Summerbee was a West Country boy from a footballing family, his uncle George having been a professional with Chester, Preston and Barrow. When he left school, he played for his home-town club Cheltenham until Swindon Town spotted his potential. He played in more than 200 games for the Wiltshire club, helping them clinch promotion from Division Three in 1962-63. Inevitably his dashing excursions along the wings caught the eyes of some of the bigger clubs and in August 1965 he became the first of Joe Mercer's signings when Manchester City paid £30,000 for his services.

He joined City at the time England manager Alf Ramsey was beginning to dispense with wingers on the international scene but he quickly adapted to the demands being made on the new breed of midfield wide men. After making his City debut in a 1-1 draw at Middlesbrough he went on in his first season to help them win the Second Division title and then in a three-year spell between 1968 and 1970 - the most successful period in the club's history - he played a significant role in City's triumphs. Though he wasn't a prolific goalscorer he did hit a hat-trick in City's 7-0 FA Cup win over Reading at Elm Park after the first match at Maine Road had ended goalless. Primarily right-footed, he made an immediate impression at Maine Road with his diligence and industry. He tackled back and shouldered his share of the defensive duties - he was a hard uncompromising player.

In the FA Cup Final of 1969, it was Summerbee who went down the right-wing avoiding the challenges of Nish and Woollett to cut the ball back from the dead-ball line for Neil Young to strike home the only goal of the game. He certainly enjoyed the limelight. A confident player on the field, deputising as a central striker when the club had injuries, he was a fashionable dresser off it and part-owner of a boutique with United's George Best. He won eight full caps for England, making his debut against Scotland in 1968. He spent ten seasons with Manchester City before he moved to Turf Moor in June 1975 for £25,000. His career later took him to Blackpool and then to the player-manager's job at Edgeley Park where his playing career ended.

HENDREY Colin J.
Keith   7 December1965

Blackburn Rovers	03.87	99	3	22
Manchester City	11.89	57	6	5
Blackburn Rovers	11.91	229	5	12

HENRY Anthony
Houghtonle Spring   26 November1957

Manchester City	12.74	68	11	6
Bolton Wanderers	09.81	70	0	22
Oldham Athletic	03.83	185	5	25
Stoke City	11.87	59	3	11
Shrewsbury Town	08.91	39	1	7

HENSON Philip M.
Manchester   30 March 1953

Manchester City	07.70	12	4	0
Swansea City (L)	07.72	1	0	0
Sheffield Wednesday	02.75	65	8	9
Stockport County	09.78	65	2	13
Rotherham United	02.80	87	5	7

HERD Alexander
Bowhill   8 November 1911

| Manchester City | 02.33 | 257 | 0 | 107 |
| Stockport County | 03.48 | 110 | 0 | 35 |

HESLOP George W.
Wallsend   1 July 1940

Newcastle United	02.59	27	0	0
Everton	03.62	10	0	0
Manchester City	09.65	159	3	1
Bury	08.72	37	0	0

HILDERSLEY Ronald
Kirkaldy   6 April 1965

Manchester City	04.83	1	0	0
Chester City(L)	01.84	9	0	0
Chester City	07.84	5	4	0
Rochdale	08.86	12	4	0
Preston North End	06.86	54	4	3
Cambridge United (L)	02.88	9	0	3
Blackburn Rovers	07.88	25	5	4
Wigan Athletic	08.90	4	0	0
Halifax Town	11.91	14	4	0

HILEY Scott P.
Plymouth   27 September 1968

Exeter City	08.86	205	5	12
Birmingham City	03.94	49	0	0
Manchester City	02.96	4	5	0
Southampton	08.98	27	2	0

Colin Bell

Colin Bell began his career with Horden Colliery Welfare where his potential was spotted by Bury. He made his league debut for the Shakers against Manchester City in February 1964 shortly before his 18th birthday. The following season he was Bury's leading goalscorer and in March 1966, after scoring 25 goals in 82 games for the Gigg Lane club, he signed for City for a fee of £45,000.

He made his City debut just three days after putting pen to paper scoring in a 2-1 win at Derby County. It was the season that Manchester City won promotion to the top flight after winning the Second Division Championship. The following season, with City back in the First Division, Bell was ever-present and scored 12 goals including the first of two hat-tricks. His three goals came in City's 3-1 home win over Stoke City. It was his form this season that led to him being selected for a variety of representative matches. He made his England debut in 1968 but it wasn't until after the 1970 World Cup that he began to establish himself in Sir Alf Ramsey's team. His non-stop running and enduring commitment in that infamous World Cup qualifying tie against Poland at Wembley sadly wasn't enough to earn England a place in the finals.

Bell had been signed for City by Joe Mercer but in 1972 when Mercer left to become general manager of Coventry City, Malcolm Allison, who had been coach since 1965, took over. Allison said of Colin Bell: 'At first he didn't seem to grasp his own freakish strength. He was the best, most powerful runner in the business.'

For a midfield player whose prodigious running was his prime quality, he was also an outstanding finisher and on 10 September 1974 he hit his second hat-trick for City as they beat Scunthorpe United 6-0 in a League Cup tie. Bell became the midfield mastermind of the young City side that won the First Division title, FA Cup, European Cup Winners' Cup and League Cup in a four year spell in the late 1960s and early 1970s.

He would have made more than his 48 appearances for England had it not been for a serious knee injury that brought his career to a premature end. The injury to his knee forced him to miss the whole of the 1976-77 season. There was though, time for one further honour, a Central League Championship medal in 1977-78 before the injury forced him to retire in August 1979. A model professional, Bell's balance and athleticism earned him the nickname 'Nijinsky' after the racehorse.

The Blues

City supporters made their way to Newcastle for what proved to be one of the most important games in the club's history.

The contest was only three minutes old when Jim Scott hit the crossbar for Newcastle but ten minutes later, City took the lead when Mike Summerbee fired home Mike Doyle's cross. Two minutes later, the Magpies were level through 'Pop' Robson.

On the half-hour mark, Tony Book cleared a Wyn Davies header off the line. Neil Young made it 2-1 for the Blues with a superb left-foot volley but just before half-Time, Sinclair equalised for Newcastle.

Three minutes into the second-half and another Neil Young goal gave City the lead. After that, the Blues tore the Magpies apart and after he had a goal disallowed for offside, Francis Lee extended City's lead in the 63rd minute, shooting past McFaul in the Newcastle goal from 12 yards.

Towards the end of the game, McNamee reduced the arrears as he scored Newcastle's third goal, but as the final whistle went, City supporters knew that their team had won the League Championship, United having lost 2-1 at home to struggling Sunderland.

The top placings in that season's First Division were as follows:

	P.	W.	D.	L.	F.	A.	Pts
Manchester City	42	26	6	10	86	43	58
Manchester United	42	24	8	10	89	55	56
Liverpool	42	22	11	9	71	40	55

The 1968-69 season began with the FA Charity Shield against the F Cup winners, West Bromwich Albion. In those days the game was played on the home ground of the League Champions and City completely outplayed the Baggies, winning 6-1. The club's League title success meant that they were allowed to participate in the European Cup for the first time in their history. City's first opponents were Turkish champions Fenerbahce, but the Blues, who were at the time lying next to the bottom of the First Division, couldn't convert any of the numerous chances that were created and the game finished goalless. The second leg was held at the National Stadium in Istanbul where, after taking the lead through Coleman, City allowed Fenerbahce to win 2-1. Though that left the Blues to concentrate solely on the domestic competitions, they had already been knocked out of the League Cup by Blackpool. In the League, City were inconsistent with victories over West Bromwich Albion (Home 5-1) Burnley (7-0) and Chelsea (4-1) being followed by draws or embarrassing defeats and at the end of the season they finished 13th.

However, the club's performances in the FA Cup were of the highest order. Third Division Luton Town were City's first victims, but the Kenilworth Road club made it difficult for the Blues and were only beaten by a Francis Lee penalty. In the fourth round, City travelled to Newcastle United but the game in which both sides had a host of chances ended goalless. In the replay at Maine Road, goals from Young and Owen gave City a 2-0 win and a place in the fifth round against Blackburn Rovers at Ewood Park. The match had to be postponed a number of times due to the poor weather and a 'flu epidemic in Blackburn, but when the game did get underway, two goals apiece from Francis Lee and Tony Coleman gave City a 4-1 win. The club's opponents in the quarter-finals were Tottenham Hotspur and though the London club fought every inch of the way, they were beaten by a Francis Lee goal in the 64th minute. The semi-final draw paired City with Everton at Villa Park. The game was goalless until the closing minutes when teenage centre-half Tommy Booth scored the winner for City with a sweetly struck left-foot shot. The club's opponents in the Final were Leicester City, who had beaten FA Cup holders West Bromwich Albion 1-0 at Hillsborough in the other semi-final.

FA Cup Final 1969
Manchester City 1 Leicester City 0

The Wembley final was the fourth season on the trot that Leicester and City had come face to face in an FA Cup tie. Just prior to the match, City captain Tony Book had been nominated joint Footballer of the Year along with Derby's Dave Mackay.

Early in the game, Leicester's Allan Clarke, then the country's most expensive player, had a powerful shot tipped to safety by Harry Dowd. The game's only goal was scored after 23 minutes when Summerbee raced down the right-wing, tricked David Nish and pushed the ball past Woollett before centring to Neil Young who blasted a left-foot drive into the top corner of Peter Shilton's net. Both teams went close during the second-half but Dowd and Shilton were in fine form and there was no further scoring. Allan Clarke was named as the Man of the Match but the Foxes were not only beaten finalists, but, like City in 1926, relegated to the Second Division.

The 1969-70 season began with the FA Charity Shield against Don Revie's Leeds United at Elland Road, a match the Yorkshire club won 2-1. In the League, City beat Sheffield Wednesday 4-1 but then lost their next three matches. It

HILL Andrew R.
Maltby — 20 January 1965

Club	Date			
Manchester United	01.83	0	0	0
Bury	07.84	264	0	10
Manchester City	12.90	91	7	6
Port Vale	08.95	96	4	1

HILL Frederick
Sheffield — 17 January 1940

Club	Date			
Bolton Wanderers	03.57	373	2	74
Halifax Town	07.69	25	0	3
Manchester City	05.70	28	7	3
Peterborough United	08.73	73	2	7

HINCE Paul F.
Manchester — 2 March 1945

Club	Date			
Manchester City	10.66	7	0	4
Charlton Athletic	02.68	23	0	2
Bury	12.68	38	0	3
Crewe Alexander	07.70	23	3	2

HINCHCLIFFE Andrew G.
Manchester — 5 February 1969

Club	Date			
Manchester City	02.86	107	5	8
Everton	07.90	170	12	6
Sheffield Wednesday	01.98	47	0	4

HODGKINSON Derek
Margate — 30 April 1944

Club	Date			
Manchester City	08.61	1	0	1
Stockport County	06.64	46	0	9

HODGSON Ronald
Birkenhead — 21 November 1922

Club	Date			
Tranmere Rovers	02.41	0	0	0
Manchester City	10.44	1	0	0
Southport	06.47	42	0	1
Crewe Alexander	02.49	31	0	0

HOEKMAN Daniel
Holland — 21 September 1964

Club	Date			
Manchester City	10.91	0	1	0

HOGAN William J.
Salford — 9 January 1924

Club	Date			
Manchester City	05.42	3	0	0
Carlisle United	09.49	191	0	27

HOLDEN Richard W.
Skipton — 9 September 1964

Club	Date			
Burnley	03.86	0	1	0
Halifax Town	09.86	66	1	12
Watford	03.88	42	0	8
Oldham Athletic	08.89	125	4	19

Tony Book

A latecomer to full-time football, Tony Book did not kick his first ball in League soccer until just before his 29th birthday. It was Malcolm Allison who discovered Book when he was the manager of Southern League Bath City. When Allison moved to Plymouth Argyle, he took Book with him and in two seasons at Home Park he missed only three games, becoming a great favourite with the Pilgrims' fans.

Allison, now Joe Mercer's assistant at Maine Road, persuaded his boss to sign Book for £17,000 and he made his debut in a 1-1 draw at Southampton in August 1966. He missed only one league game in his first two seasons with City before his career looked to be over following an Achilles tendon injury late in 1968. However, upon his return to first team action, City had a great cup run which ended when they beat Leicester City at Wembley in the 1969 FA Cup Final. Book was voted Footballer of the Year with Derby County's Dave Mackay at the end of the season.

He was back at Wembley the following year, carrying off the Football League Cup and seven weeks later, the European Cup Winners' Cup as City beat Gornik Zabrze 2-1.

Book retired from playing in 1973 and joined City's coaching staff. He became assistant to Ron Saunders and when Saunders left in 1974, Book took over as City manager. He soon found some success as a manager when City won the Football League Cup in 1976 and were runners-up in the League in 1976-77. In the summer of 1979, Book was made general manager with Allison returning as team manager and he later had an important behind-the-scenes-role. Working with the younger players he found some outstanding youngsters to win the FA Youth Cup for the first time in 1986. In November 1989 he was appointed caretaker-manager after Mel Machin was sacked and became first-team coach under Peter Reid in the early 1990s.

Manchester City	07.92	49	1	3
Oldham Athletic	10.93	46	14	9
Blackpool	09.95	19	3	2

HOPKINS Robert A.

Birmingham	25 October 1961			
Aston Villa	07.79	1	2	1
Birmingham City	03.83	123	0	20
Manchester City	08.86	7	0	1
West Bromwich Albion	10.86	81	2	11
Birmingham City	03.89	43	7	9
Shrewsbury Town	06.91	18	9	3

HORLOCK Kevin

Bexley	1 November 1972			
West Ham United	07.91	0	0	0
SwindonTown	08.92	151	12	22
Manchester City	01.97	79	1	18

HORNE Stanley F.

Clanfield	17 December 1944			
Aston Villa	12.61	6	0	0
Manchester City	09.65	48	2	0
Fulham	02.69	73	6	0
ChesterCity	08.73	17	1	0
Rochdale	12.73	48	0	5

HORRIDGE Peter

Manchester	31 May 1934			
Manchester City	11.52	3	0	0
Crewe Alexandra	06.59	0	0	0

HORSWILL Michael F.

Annfield Plain	6 March 1953			
Sunderland	03.70	68	1	3
Manchester City	03.74	11	3	0
Plymouth Argyle	06.75	98	4	3
Hull City	07.78	82	2	6
Carlisle United	08.83	1	0	0

HOYLAND Jamie W.

Sheffield	23 January 1966			
Manchester City	11.83	2	0	0
Bury	07.86	169	3	25
Sheffield United	07.90	72	17	6
Bristol City (L)	03.94	6	0	0
Burnley	10.94	77	10	4
Carlisle United(L)	11.97	5	0	0
Scarborough	08.98	44	0	3

HUGHES Michael E.

Larne	2 August 1971			
Manchester City	08.88	25	1	1
West Ham United (L)	11.94	15	2	2
West Ham United (L)	10.95	28	0	0

Francis Lee

Francis Lee made his league debut for Bolton Wanderers as a 16-year-old amateur in November 1960 after playing in only eight Central League games. He partnered 35-year-old Nat Lofthouse on the right-wing in a 3-1 victory over Manchester City. It was an eventful debut for Lee as he scored a goal and got booked !

He signed professional forms for Bolton in May 1961 but his volatile nature caused problems off the field when he refused to play after being dropped to the Bolton 'A' team.

Things were patched up and though clubs were keen to sign him following a string of transfer requests, Lee stayed with Bolton until the beginning of the 1967-68 season.

In October 1967, at the age of 23, he signed for Manchester City and made his league debut in a 2-0 home win over Wolverhampton Wanderers. During his eight years with Bolton he had scored over 100 goals and was rarely out of the headlines. He soon became a firm favourite with the Maine Road fans and was one of the successes in a City team that enjoyed one of the greatest eras in the club's history.

By the time he went to City, he was playing in a more orthodox striking role. Franny Lee was a bustling, sturdy, little striker. He had a barrel chest and though slightly portly, he was one of the most tenacious and effective of strikers, scoring many goals. His three hat-tricks in his time at Maine Road included a spectacular threesome in the Manchester derby at Old Trafford in December 1970. His others came in the 5-2 win over Wolves in January 1972 and in a 4-0 defeat of Walsall in a League Cup second round replay played at Old Trafford after the first two matches failed to produce a goal.

Francis Lee won a lot of penalties for City and wasn't really fussy about how he won them. City won so many penalties during the early 1970s many of them awarded for fouls on Franny, that it became a topical talking point. In the European Cup Winnes' Cup Final of 1970 against Gornik Zabrze of Poland, he hit the ball so hard and straight into the net, that it needed a close study of an action-replay to check the ball had not gone through Kostka the goalkeeper's body !

In 1971-72, Lee topped the First Division scoring charts with 33 goals including 15 fom the penalty spot. For this achievement he was awarded the bronze boot in the Golden Boot competition.

Lee was also a vital part of Sir Alf Ramsey's England squad and had gone to Mexico to defend the World Cup in 1970. He scored 10 goals in 27 appearances for England. In August 1974 he left City to join Derby County for £110,000 and in his first season at the Baseball Ground, helped the Rams win the League Championship. He retired in 1976 and by then his paper business which he started as a player with Bolton was a great success and eventually secured him millionaire status. In February 1994 he became chairman of Manchester City before resigning during the 1997-98 season.

The Blues

was this inconsistency that dogged their season and they ended the campaign in 10th place though they did complete the 'double' over United, winning 4-0 at Maine Road and 2-1 at Old Trafford.

In the Football League Cup, the Blues beat Southport 3-0 to set up a third round tie against Bill Shankly's Liverpool at Maine Road. The Anfield men had already beaten City twice in the League but it was a different story in the League Cup. Mike Doyle fired City ahead in the 11th minute from fully 35 yards and though Alun Evans equalised for Liverpool, Neil Young put the Blues back in the lead. Ian Bowyer made it 3-1 to City before Liverpool reduced the arrears and though the Merseyside club lay siege to the City goal, they held on to record a memorable 3-2 victory. In the fourth round, goals by Lee and Bell ensured City of a place in the quarter-finals as they beat Everton 2-0. City's opponents were Queen's Park Rangers, but the London club were well beaten by the Maine Road club 3-0 with Bell (2) and Summervbee the scorers. This City victory set up a two-legged semi-final against rivals Manchester United. In the first leg at Maine Road, the Blues dominated the first-half and went in at the interval 1-0 up through a Colin Bell goal. In the 66th minute Bobby Charlton equalised for the Reds and though City pressed hard for a second goal, Alex Stepney kept them at bay. Then in the 88th minute, Francis Lee was brought down in the penalty area by Ian Ure. World Cup referee Jack Taylor awarded a spot-kick and Lee struck the ball low to Stepney's right and City had won 2-1. In the return game at Old Trafford a fortnight later, a crowd of 63,418 saw Ian Bowyer extend City's aggregate lead. Paul

Edwards pulled one back for the Reds and then former City player Denis Law made it 2-1 for United on the night and 3-3 on aggregate. As the minutes ticked by, extra-time seemed the likely outcome but with just eight minutes to go, the tie was settled when fate took a hand. Willie Morgan fouled Ian Bowyer on the edge of the Reds' penalty area. The referee signalled an indirect free-kick and Francis Lee thundered in a direct shot at goal. Amazingly, United's 'keeper Stepney parried the shot but only to Mike Summerbee who scored the goal that gave City a 4-3 aggregate win and a place in the final against West Bromwich Albion.

League Cup Final 1970
Manchester City 2
West Bromwich Albion 1

The Blues, who had just returned from a European Cup Winners' Cup match with the Portuguese side Academica Coimbra, exhausted, turned out on a muddy pitch at Wembley in bitterly cold conditions. City once again wore their successful black and red striped shirts but found themselves a goal down after five minutes when Albion's England international centre-forward, Jeff Astle headed home Ray Wilson's cross. City dominated the rest of the half with Doyle and Oakes running the midfield. It was Mike Doyle who equalised for City in the 60th minute when Colin Bell headed across the face of the Albion goal for the City midfielder to slam the ball home. Both sides chased a winner but there was no further scoring in normal time. City dominated the period of extra-time and in the 102nd minute, Glyn Pardoe emerged as the club's match-winner as his shot beat John Osborne in the Albion goal. So City had

A Concise Post War History of Manchester City

won the League Cup in the first season that all 92 League clubs had taken part in the competition.

In the European Cup Winners' Cup, the Blues travelled to Spain to play Athletic Bilbao and though they dominated the early exchanges, found themselves 2-0 down after quarter-of-an-hour. Neil Young pulled a goal back before the Spaniards extended their lead. Tommy Booth reduced the arrears before an own goal by Bilbao's captain Luis Echeberria levelled the scores. In the second leg, City cruised into the next round with a 3-0 win with goals from Bell, Oakes and Bowyer. The club repeated that scoreline in their second round tie at SK Lierse of Belgium with Colin Bell and two from Francis Lee the scorers. At Maine Road both Bell and Lee scored two goals apiece and Mike Summerbee added another in a 5-0 rout. The quarter-final tie paired City with Portuguese Cup holders Academica Coimbra, the first leg in Portugal which was goalless, being played just three days before the club's League Cup Final appearance. The return at Maine Road also ended goalless after 90 minutes and went into extra-time, where a Tony Towers goal was enough to take the club into the semi-final of the competition. City's opponents were the German side Schalke 04 and they beat the Blues 1-0 in the first leg at Gelsenkirchen. However, City had dominated that first meeting and were in confident mood for the return leg at Maine Road. The Blues completeley overran the Germans, winning 5-1 with goals from Young (2) Doyle, Lee and Bell to set up a European Cup Winners' Cup Final against Gornik Zabrze of Poland.

European Cup Winners' Cup Final 1970
Manchester City 2 Gornik Zabrze 1

West Ham United	08.96	33	5	3
Wimbledon	09.97	57	2	6

HUTCHISON Thomas
Cardenden   22 September 1947
Blackpool	02.68	163	2	10
Coventry City	10.72	312	2	24
Manchester City	10.80	44	2	4
Burnley	08.83	92	0	4
Swansea City	07.85	163	15	9

IMMEL Elke
Germany   27 November1960
Manchester City	08.95	42	0	0

INGEBRIGTSEN Kare
Sweden   11 November 1965
Manchester City	08.94	4	10	0

INGRAM Rae
Manchester   6 December 1974
Manchester City	07.93	18	5	0
Macclesfield Town	03.98	28	6	0

JACKSON Gary A.
Swinton   30 September 1964
Manchester City	10.81	6	2	0
Exeter City	09.85	34	1	2

JACKSON Harold
Blackburn   30 December 1918
Burnley	01.42	0	0	0
Manchester City	06.46	8	0	2
Preston North End	12.47	18	0	5
Blackburn Rovers	12.48	1	0	0
ChesterCity	07.49	21	0	10

JEFFRIES Derek
Manchester   22 March 1951
Manchester City	08.68	64	9	0
Crystal Palace	09.73	107	0	1
Peterborough Utd (L)	10.76	7	0	0
Millwall (L)	03.77	10	1	0
Chester City	07.77	116	5	2

JOBSON Richard
Holderness   9 May 1963
Watford	11.82	26	2	4
Hull City	02.85	219	21	7
Oldham Athletic	08.90	188	1	10
Leeds United	10.95	22	0	1
Southend United (L)	01.98	8	0	1
Manchester City	03.98	6	0	1

The Blues

Tommy Booth   Hailing from the Middleton estate of Langley, Tommy Booth had something of a meteoric rise to fame after making his debut for the Blues in a 1-1 home draw against Arsenal in October 1968.

He ended his first season with City by scoring the winning goal in the FA Cup semi-final against Everton at Villa Park. He also won an England Under-23 cap in that 1968-69 season, his performances prompting Joe Mercer to describe him as being like 'Stan Cullis and Neil Franklin rolled into one.'

Tommy Booth was Manchester City's first-choice centre-half for seven seasons, missing very few games. However, when England international centre-half Dave Watson joined the Blues from Sunderland for £275,000, Booth found his appearances in the heart of the City defence limited. Following Colin Bell's injury, Booth showed his versatility by moving into midfield and producing some very effective performances.

During his City career, Booth won several honours - an FA Cup winners' medal, a European Cup Winners' Cup medal and two League Cup winners' medals as well as playing in a third League Cup Final when City went down 2-1 to Wolves. He had appeared in 478 League and Cup games for the Blues when he was allowed to join Preston North End in September 1981 for £30,000. He had made 84 appearances for the Deepdale club when in April 1985 he was appointed the club's manager. He was not a great success as manager and was dismissed after North End entered one of the worst spells in

On a very wet night in Vienna, City took the lead at the Prater Stadium in the 12th minute when the Gornik 'keeper Kostka failed to hold Francis Lee's powerful shot and Neil Young followed up to put the Blues ahead. City went further ahead just before half-time when scorer Neil Young was brought down inside the penalty area and Francis Lee stepped up to crash the ball into the roof of the net. The Poles pulled a goal back in the 68th minute when their captain Oslizlo fired past Corrigan but the Blues held their nerve and when the final whistle went, City had become the first English club side to win a major domestic and European trophy in the same season.

In only five seasons, the Mercer-Allison combination had guided the Blues to five trophies - the League Championship, League Cup, European Cup Winners' Cup, Second Division Championship and FA Cup.

City were determined to build on these successes and started the 1970-71 season in fine style. They were unbeaten in the League until 26 September when they went down 2-0 to Tottenham Hotspur at White Hart Lane. At this time the Blues were in second place in the table, just behind Leeds United, but then injuries and events off the field began to alter the situation. Booth and Oakes were both nursing cartilage problems whilst Glyn Pardoe suffered a fractured leg following a tackle by George Best in the Manchester derby on 12 December. However, they did beat United 4-1 that day with Francis Lee netting a hat-trick, but sadly the Blues failed to score in 17 of their 42 league games and ended the season in 11th place.

The club's bid to retain the League Cup ended at the first hurdle when they were beaten 2-1 at Carlisle United.

JOHNSON David R.

Liverpool	23 October 1951			
Everton	04.69	47	3	11
Ipswich Town	11.72	134	3	35
Liverpool	08.76	128	20	55
Everton	08.82	32	8	4
Barnsley	02.84	4	0	1
Manchester City	03.84	4	2	1
Preston North End	10.84	20	4	3

JOHNSON Jeffrey D.

Cardiff	26 November 1953			
Manchester City	12.70	4	2	0
Swansea City	07.72	37	2	4
Crystal Palace	12.73	82	5	4
Sheffield Wednesday	07.76	175	5	6
Newport County	08.81	34	0	2
Gillingham	09.82	85	3	4
Port Vale	07.85	10	0	1

JOHNSON Nigel M.

Rotherham	23 June 1964			
Rotherham United	06.82	89	0	1
Manchester City	06.85	4	0	0
Rotherham United	07.87	141	3	7

JOHNSTONE Robert

Selkirk	7 September 1929			
Manchester City	03.55	124	0	42
Oldham Athletic	10.60	143	03	6

JONES Christopher H.

Jersey	18 April 1956			
Tottenham Hotspur	05.73	149	15	37
Manchester City	09.82	3	0	0
Crystal Palace	11.82	18	0	3
Charlton Athletic	09.83	17	6	2
Leyton Orient	09.84	106	1	19

JONES Christopher M.N.

Altrincham	19 November 1945			
Manchester City	05.64	6	1	2
Swindon Town	07.68	49	19	18
Oldham Athletic (L)	01.72	3	0	1
Walsall	02.72	54	5	14
York City	06.73	94	1	34
Huddersfield Town	08.76	9	5	2
Doncaster Rovers	07.77	14	6	4
Darlington (L)	01.78	14	2	3
Rochdale	12.78	51	5	19

JONES William J.B.

Liverpool	6 June 1924			
Manchester City	05.48	3	0	0

Joe Corrigan

Joe Corrigan's first team debut for Manchester City was in the League Cup tie against Blackpool at Maine Road in October 1967 but he had to wait until March 1969 for his Football League debut at Portman Road, Ipswich beating City 2-1.

In his early days he was always in the shadow of Harry Dowd and Ken Mulhearn though when he did get a chance he was inconsistent. Despite this unimpressive start to his League career, he fought hard to establish himself but faced another crisis of confidence when in 1975, City signed Motherwell's Keith MacRae for £100,000. Out of favour with the then City manager Ron Saunders, he asked for a transfer and was transfer-listed in February 1974. However, once again the 6ft 4 ins goalkeeper buckled down and won back his first team place, going on to serve City for a further nine years. Manchester City have had three outstanding 'keepers since the war - Swift, Trautmann and Corrigan. I'm sure if he'd been around at a different time than Ray Clemence and Peter Shilton he would have won far more than the nine caps he did. He won his first in 1976, coming on as a substitute against Italy in New York and his last against Iceland in 1982. He also played in an unofficial game for England against Atletico Bilbao in 1981, plus ten appearances for England 'B'.

His best season for City was 1976-77 when he only conceded 34 goals in his 42 League appearances, keeping 22 clean sheets.

He won League Cup honours in 1970 and 1976 and a European Cup Winners' Cup medal in 1970 when City beat Gornik Zabrze 2-1. When City played Tottenham Hotspur at Wembley in the 1981 FA Cup Final, Corrigan had looked unbeatable - the game ending 1-1. For his heroics between the posts, Corrigan was named Man-of-the-Match, though he was beaten three times in the replay as the North London side won 3-2.

Corrigan played in 592 League and Cup games for City, making him second only to Alan Oakes in terms of the number of first team games for City.

In March 1983, City transferred him to Seattle Sounders in the NASL for £30,000. He later returned to these shores to play for Brighton and Hove Albion, Norwich City and Stoke City before retiring.

The Blues

In the European Cup Winners' Cup, City faced Linfield of Northern Ireland and in a closely fought game at Maine Road, had to settle for a 1-0 win with Colin Bell grabbing the all-important goal. The Blues lost the return leg in Belfast 2-1 and once again had Bell to thank as his late goal took City through to the next round on the away goals rule. They travelled to Budapest to play Honved and though Francis Lee scored the only goal of the game, City dominated proceedings. In the second leg at Maine Road, goals from Bell and Lee helped City win 2-0 on a night when the appalling conditions almost caused the game to be abandoned. In the quarter-final, City faced last season's Cup Winners' Cup Final opponents, Gornik Zabrze but were beaten 2-0 in

Willie Donachie

Manchester City were the reigning League Champions when Willie Donachie joined the club as a junior from Glasgow United in 1968. In those days he was a midfield player but with the Blues going on to win the FA Cup in 1969 and the League Cup in 1970 he found it difficult to break into the team, though he did make his debut in February 1970 in a 1-1 home draw against Nottingham Forest.

Early in 1971 he took over from Alan Oakes for a time, but it was as a long term replacement at left-back for broken leg victim Glyn Pardoe that Donachie established himself.

His skill and class were soon noticed by the international selectors and in April 1972 he won the first of 35 caps when he played against Peru at Hampden Park.

Donachie was a virtual ever-present during his time at Maine Road, all of which was spent in the First Division. He played in two League Cup Finals, going down to Wolves in 1974 but collected a winners' medal against Newcastle United in 1976. He also played in every game when City were beaten to the League Championship by a single point by Liverpool in 1976-77.

After his position came under threat, City accepted £200,000 from NASL club Portland Timbers. After a brief return to help Norwich City win promotion from the Second Division in 1982 he returned to Portland before joining Burnley. He failed to prevent the Clarets from being relegated but after two seasons at Turf Moor he joined Oldham Athletic where he was later made player-coach.

His partnership with Joe Royle was a major factor in Oldham's success in recent years. When Royle was appointed Everton manager, Donachie was his choice as his assistant, the two of them guiding the Merseysiders to FA Cup success against Manchester United in 1995. The popular Scot is now back at his beloved Maine Road as the club's head coach.

Poland. At Maine Road, City won 2-0 with goals from Mellor and Doyle and so with the aggregate score at 2-2, a third game was arranged in Copenhagen. The Blues dominated the match, beating the Poles 3-1 with Booth, Lee and Young the City goalscorers. In the semi-finals, City found themselves facing FA Cup winners' Chelsea, a team that they had beaten 3-0 in the FA Cup before being knocked out by Arsenal in the next round. The first leg at Stamford Bridge saw a City side decimated by injuries go down 1-0 with Joe Corrigan in goal producing a number of outstanding saves. The gaint 'keeper was missing from the second leg, as were other City players and though the youngsters who turned out gave of their

Chester City	06.51	29	0	5
KARL Stefan				
Germany	3 February 1970			
Manchester City	03.94	4	2	1
KAVELASHVILA Mikhail				
Tbilisi,Georgia	22 July 1971			
Manchester City	03.96	9	19	3
KEEGAN Gerard A.				
Walkden	3 October1955			
Manchester City	03.73	32	5	2
Oldham Athletic	02.79	139	5	5
Mansfield Town	10.83	18	0	1
Rochdale	07.84	2	0	0
KELLY Raymond				
Athlone	29 December 1976			
Manchester City	08.94	1	0	0
Wrexham (L)	10.97	5	1	1
Wrexham (L)	03.98	0	4	0
KENNEDY Robert				
Motherwell	23 June 1937			
Manchester City	07.61	216	3	9
Grimsby Town	03.69	84	0	1
KERNAGHAN Alan N.				
Otley	25 April 1967			
Middlesbrough	03.85	1724016		
Charlton Athletic (L)	01.91	13	0	0
Manchester City	09.93	55	8	1
Bolton Wanderers (L)	08.94	9	0	2
Bradford City (L)	02.96	5	0	0
KERR Andrew				
Cumnock	29 June 1932			
Manchester City	06.59	10	0	0
Sunderland	04.63	18	0	5
KERR David W.				
Dumfries	6 September 1974			
Manchester City	09.91	4	2	0
Mansfield Town (L)	09.95	4	1	0
Mansfield Town	07.96	46	16	4
KEVAN Derek T.				
Ripon	6 March 1935			
Bradford Park Avenue	10.52	15	0	8
West Bromwich Albion	07.53	262	0	157
Chelsea	03.63	701		
Manchester City	08.63	67	0	48
Crystal Palace	07.65	21	0	5
Peterborough United	03.66	16	1	2

Rodney Marsh

Rodney Marsh was the clown-prince of football, a flamboyant and precocious talent who should have won more than the nine England caps he gained. He began his career with Fulham and scored a magnificent volleyed goal on his league debut as the Cottagers beat Aston Villa 1-0. His career was making rapid progress when he sustained a serious injury at Leicester in February 1965 which left him partially deaf. After losing form he was sold to Queen's Park Rangers for £15,000 and played an important role in Rangers' rise from the Third to the First Division. He also won a League Cup winners' medal whilst at Loftus Road, scoring one of the goals in a sensational victory over West Bromwich Albion. In March 1972 Manchester City paid £200,000 to bring Marsh to Maine Road and he made his debut in a 1-0 home win over Chelsea. With Marsh in the side, City became a joy to watch as his imaginative play set up a host of chances for his team-mates. Though not a prolific scorer, he did manage one hat-trick for the club as the Blues beat York City 4-1 in the League Cup competition of 1973-74. That season he won another League Cup medal as City lost 2-1 to Wolves in the final.

Marsh next moved to the United States to join Tampa Bay Rowdies and later managed them before retiring from playing. He returned to Fulham briefly in September 1976 to team up with George Best but injury dogged his stay.

Luton Town	12.66	11	0	4
Stockport County	03.67	38	2	10

KIDD Brian
Manchester 29 May 1949

Manchester United	06.66	195	8	52
Arsenal	08.74	77	0	30
Manchester City	07.76	97	1	44
Everton	03.79	40	0	12
Bolton Wanderers	05.80	40	3	14

KINKLADZE Georgiou
Tbilisi, Georgia 6 November 1973

Manchester City	08.95	105	1	20

KINSEY Stephen
Manchester 2 January 1963

Manchester City	01.80	87	14	15
Chester City	09.82	3	0	1
Chesterfield	11.82	3	0	0
Rochdale (N/C)	10.91	3	3	1

KIRKMAN Alan J.
Bolton 21 June 1936

Manchester City	02.56	7	0	
Rotherham United	03.59	143	0	58
Newcastle United	09.63	5	0	1
Scunthorpe United	12.63	32	0	5
Torquay United	07.65	58	1	8
Workington	01.67	56	0	3

LAKE Paul A.
Denton 28 October 1968

Manchester City	05.87	106	4	7

LANGLEY Kevin J.
St Helens 24 May 1964

Wigan Athletic	05.82	156	4	6
Everton	07.86	16	0	2
Manchester City	03.87	9	0	0
Chester City (L)	01.88	9	0	0
Birmingham City	03.88	74	2	2
Wigan Athletic	09.90	151	3	4

LAW Denis
Aberdeen 24 February 1940

Huddersfield Town	02.57	81	0	16
Manchester City	03.60	44	0	21
Manchester United	08.62	305	4	171
Manchester City	07.73	22	2	9

LEE Francis H.
Westhoughton 29 April 1944

Bolton Wanderers	05.61	189	0	92
Manchester City	10.67	248	1	112

The Blues

best, it was Chelsea who scored the game's only goal to win 2-0 on aggregate.

The 1970-71 season also saw the club the subject of a take-over bid with a consortium led by Oldham double-glazing tycoon, Joe Smith. However, following a board meeting, Frank Johnson, who it had been said was willing to sell his shares, decided against doing so when learning of the identity of two of Smith's associates ! Sadly though it was also the beginning of the break-up of the relationship between Joe Mercer and Malcolm Allison as both men were on different sides of the take-over.

In April 1971, a certain Peter Swales along with Joe Smith joined the City board and though the take-over was not resolved, the changes in the boardroom meant differing roles for Mercer and Allison. Joe Mercer became General Manager whilst Allison was given the title of Team Manager.

Despite a 1-0 defeat against Leeds United on the opening day of the 1971-72 season, City, whose playing surface was now the largest in the Football League, after it was widened in the close season, won four home games in succession to move into fourth place after a month of the season. By the time of the Maine Road derby match in November, the Blues had moved up to third place. A crowd of 63,326 saw the sides play out a 3-3 draw with Francis Lee, who scored a record 13 penalties that season, opening the scoring from the spot. In a game full of incident, City had Mike Summerbee to thank for grabbing a last-minute equaliser. By the turn of the year, the Blues had moved into second place in the League, just a point behind leaders Manchester United. City went top of the League at the end of January 1972 after a Francis

Lee hat-trick helped them beat Wolves 5-2. City were four points clear of second-placed Leeds United and after signing Rodney Marsh from Queen's Park Rangers for £200,000, were confident they could go on to win the Championship. However, Marsh wasn't fully fit and both his and the club's performances suffered. Despite scoring two goals in a 3-1 win at West Ham United, by the time of the Old Trafford derby, the new-signing was on the bench, the first time he hadn't made the starting line-up. The Blues were 2 1 up with Lee having scored both goals when Marsh replaced the injured Doyle and with virtually his first touch of the ball, he increased City's lead. With just two games of the season remaining, the Blues were one point behind leaders Derby County. Also Leeds United and Liverpool were in contention for the Championship as both sides had a game in hand over the clubs above them. Sadly City lost 2-1 to Ipswich Town in the penultimate game of the season and though they beat Derby County 2-0 to go top of the table, they had to wait for a further 12 days before the other three sides completed their fixtures. In the end, the Rams won the title with City in fourth place on the same number of points as runners-up Leeds United and third-placed Liverpool.

	P	W	D	L	F	A	Pts
Derby County	42	24	10	8	69	33	58
Leeds United	42	24	9	9	73	31	57
Liverpool	42	24	9	9	64	30	57
Manchester City	42	23	11	8	77	45	57

In the close season, Joe Mercer left Maine Road to become General Manager of Coventry City.

Prior to the start of the 1972-73 seson, City were invited to play in the FA Charity Shield and in beating Aston

Villa 1-0, at Villa Park in front of a 34,860 crowd brought the award to Maine Road just four yaers after last winning the trophy.

With Allison in the managerial seat, the season started poorly with City winning only two of their first eight league games. The Blues were bottom of the League, a point behind Manchester United, but by the time of the Maine Rad derby match on 18 November 1972, City had moved off the foot of the table and beat the Reds 3-0. The club returned to European action but were knocked out of the UEFA Cup in the first round, losing 4-3 on aggregate to Valencia. A week later, the Blues, who had beaten Rochdale in round two, were knocked out of the League Cup by Fourth Division Bury. The FA Cup brought some joy as City beat Stoke 3-2 in the third round to set up a meeting with Liverpool. After a goalless draw at Anfield, goals from Bell and Booth gave City a 2-0 win. The fifth round saw City paired with Sunderland at Maine Road. In an entertaining game in which Tony Towers was sent-off, the Blues were trailing 2-1 with just minutes to go when Jim Montgomery, the Wearsiders' 'keeper, back-heeled the ball into his own net for City's equaliser. Even then both teams had the chance to win it but the score remained 2-2. In the replay at Roker Park, the Second Division side won 3-1 and went on to win the trophy, beating Leeds United in the final.

At the end of March, Malcolm Allison left Maine Road to take over the reins at Crystal Palace. Johnny Hart acted as the club's caretaker-manager and lifted the Blues to 11th place.

During the summer of 1973, Denis Law rejoined City from rivals Manchester United who had given him a free transfer at the end of the 1972-73 season. The campaign opened with the

DerbyCounty	08.74	62	0	24

LEE Stuart F.

Manchester	11 February 1953			
Bolton Wanderers	02.71	77	8	20
Wrexham	11.75	46	8	12
Stockport County	08.78	49	0	21
Manchester City	09.79	6	1	2

LEIGH Peter

Wythenshawe	4 March 1939			
Manchester City	08.57	2	0	0
Crewe Alexandra	06.61	430	0	3

LEIVERS William E.

Bolsover	29 January 1932			
Chesterfield	02.50	27	0	0
Manchester City	11.53	250	0	4
Doncaster Rovers	07.64	24	0	1

LEMAN Dennis

Newcastle	1 December 1954			
Manchester City	12.71	10	7	1
Sheffield Wednesday	12.76	89	15	9
Wrexham	02.82	17	0	1
Scunthorpe United	08.82	38	0	3

LENNON Neil F.

Lurgan	25 June 1971			
Manchester City	08.89	1	0	0
Crewe Alexandra	08.90	142	5	15
Leicester City	02.96	123	1	5

LESTER Michael J.

Manchester	4 August 1954			
Oldham Athletic	08.72	26	1	2
Manchester City	11.73	1	1	0
Stockport County	08.75	8	1	1
Grimsby Town	11.77	45	3	10
Barnsley	10.79	64	0	11
Exeter City	08.81	18	1	6
Bradford City	02.82	46	3	2
Scunthorpe United	03.83	106	0	9
Hartlepool United	01.86	11	0	1
Stockport County	09.86	11	0	0
Blackpool	12.87	11	0	1

LILLIS Mark A.

Manchester	17 January 1960			
Huddersfield Town	07.78	199	7	56
Manchester City	06.85	39	0	11
DerbyCounty	08.86	6	9	1
Aston Villa	09.87	30	1	4
Scunthorpe United	09.89	62	6	23
Stockport County	09.91	9	2	2

The Blues

Dennis Tueart

Dennis Tueart was a regular in the Sunderland team relegated from the top flight in 1970 and spent the rest of his Roker Park career in the Second Division. The highlight was undoubtedly the Wearsiders' memorable victory over Leeds United in the FA Cup Final of 1973. During Sunderland's first-ever European campaign in the Cup Winners' Cup of 1973-74, Tueart scored in both legs of the first round tie against Vasas Budapest but after the club were beaten in a later round by Sporting Lisbon, Tueart left Roker Park to join Manchester City for £275,000, then a record fee for both clubs.

City had timed their approach well just as Tueart was approaching the peak of his form and after making his debut in a goalless Manchester derby, he won international recognition for the first time. He represented the Football League against the Scottish League and scored in a 5-0 win at Maine Road. In December 1974 he was chosen as an over-age player in England's Under-23 side to meet Scotland at Aberdeen and scored twice in a 3-0 victory. In May 1975, at the end of his first season with City, he was selected for England in a European Championship qualifier against Cyprus, going on to score two goals in six appearances for his country.

He was City's top scorer in 1975-76 with 24 League and Cup goals including a hat-trick in a 6-1 League Cup win over Norwich City as the Blues went on to lift the trophy. In the final against Newcastle United, Tueart clinched victory for City with a spectacular overhead kick, a goal that has rightly been played endlessly on television.

Tueart's best season in terms of goals scored was 1976-77 when his 18 goals helped City finish runners-up in the First Division to Liverpool. The following season he netted three hat-tricks in his total of 12 goals as City beat Aston Villa (Away 4-1) Chelsea (Home 6-2) and Newcastle United (Home 4-0). Then in February 1978 he was lured to America to join New York Cosmos for £250,000. Tueart returned to Maine Road early in 1980 and although no longer a regular in City's side, collected an FA Cup runners-up medal at the end of the replayed final against Tottenham Hotspur. He left City in the summer of 1983 and after spells with Stoke and Burnley he briefly turned out for Irish League club Derry City before hanging up his boots. Tueart is now back at Maine Road as one of the club's directors.

club having accepted another invitation to take part in the Charity Shield but despite having a lot of possession, City lost 1-0 at home to Burnley. The first league game of the season saw Law score twice in a 3-1 win over Birmingham City, the Scottish international going on to score nine goals in 22 league games. In October 1973, Peter Swales was appointed club chairman and it wasn't too long before he had to appoint a new manager as Johnny Hart quit after six months in charge due to ill-health. His replacement was Ron Saunders and though league performances under the former Norwich manager didn't really improve, the League Cup was a different story. The Blues had already beaten

LINACRE William

Chesterfield	10 August 1924			
Chesterfield	02.44	22	0	3
Manchester City	10.47	75	0	6
Middlesbrough	09.49	31	0	2
Hartlepool United	08.53	89	0	10
Mansfield Town	10.55	13	0	0

LISTER Herbert F.

Manchester	4 October 1939			
Manchester City	11.57	2	0	0
Oldham Athletic	10.60	135	0	81
Rochdale	01.65	56	0	16
Stockport County	01.67	16	0	11

LITTLE Roy

Manchester	1 June 1931			
Manchester City	08.49	168	0	2
Brighton & Hove Albion	10.58	83	0	0
Crystal Palace	05.61	38	0	1

LOMAS Stephen M.

Hanover, Germany	18 January 1974			
Manchester City	01.91	102	9	8
West Ham United	03.97	70	0	3

LOMAX Geoffrey W.

Droylsden	6 July 1964			
Manchester City	07.81	23	2	1
Wolverhampton Wands (L)	10.85	5	0	0
Carlisle United	12.85	37	0	0
Rochdale	07.87	70	1	0

McADAMS William J.

Belfast	20 January 1934			
Manchester City	12.53	127	0	62
Bolton Wanderers	09.60	44	0	26
Leeds United	12.61	11	0	3
Brentford	07.62	75	0	36
Queen's Park Rangers	09.64	33	0	13
Barrow	07.66	53	0	9

McALINDEN Robert J.

Salford	22 May 1946			
Manchester City	05.64	1	0	0
Port Vale	09.65	0	0	0
Bournemouth	09.76	1	0	0

McCARTHY Michael J.

Barnsley	7 February 1959			
Barnsley	07.77	272	0	7
Manchester City	12.83	140	0	2
Millwall	03.90	31	4	2

The Blues

Walsall at Old Trafford 4-0 after two goalless draw, Carlisle United (Away 1-0) and drawn 0-0 at York City before Saunders' arrival. In the replay City beat York 4-1 with Rodney Marsh grabbing a hat-trick. They then travelled to Highfield Road to play Coventry City in the fifth round. In a game which could have gone either way, the sides drew 2-2 in front of a Wednesay afternoon crowd of only 12,661. In the replay at Maine Road, also played in the afternoon, City came from behind to win 4-2. In the first-leg of the semi-final, a Tommy Booth goal gave City a 1-1 draw at Third Division Plymouth Argyle. In the second-leg, City proved too strong for the Home Park club, winning 2-0 with goals from Bell and Lee. In the final against Wolverhampton Wanderers, City had the better of the early exchanges but it was the Molineux club who scored the opening goal when Kenny Hibbitt's mis-hit shot crept in at the far post just two minutes before the interval. City drew level on the hour when Colin Bell converted Rodney Marsh's cross and came close to taking the lead as both Lee and Marsh brought some fine saves out of Wolves' 'keeper Pierce. There were just five minutes left when John Richards scored to put Wolves 2-1 up and seal victory.

Not long after that defeat, Saunders signed Dennis Tueart and Mick Horswill from Sunderland with City's Tony Towers going in the opposite direction. Tuaert's debut was in the Manchester derby and though the game was goalless, it wasn't without incident as refeee Clive Thomas was forced to take both sides off the field until Mike Doyle and United's Lou Macari had accepted his decision to send them off !

Shortly after this game, Saunders was sacked and replaced by his assistant,

Tony Book. He was just what the club needed and with him in charge, the Blues ended the season in 14th place, four points clear of the relegation zone. The final match of the season was the Old Trafford derby with Denis Law playing his last game in league football. The Reds were struggling to avoid relegation and needed to beat City to stand any chance of survival. A crowd of 56,996 saw the game which looked destined to end in a draw when suddenly, with just nine minutes remaining, a clever back-heel from Law evaded Alex Stepney in the United goal to give the Blues a 1-0 win and help send the Old Trafford club into Division Two !

Before the start of the 1974-75 season, Book had signed Asa Hartford from West Bromwich Albion for £250,000, whilst Francis Lee moved on to Derby County. Rodney Marsh had been made skipper and it was his memorable goal - an overhead kick against Queen's Park Rangers - that took the Blues into second place in Division One. By November the club were top of the league but sadly this successful run wasn't sustained due to a number of injuries and suspensions. Also the club only managed to win two away games and so had to settle for eighth place at the end of the season. In that season's League Cup, City beat Scunthopre United who were bottom of the Fourth Division, 6-0 before being paired with Manchester United in the next round. The Reds won this battle 1-0 courtesy of a Gerry Daly penalty. In the FA Cup, the Blues were drawn away to Newcastle United but the Magpies' crowd problems meant that the venue had to be switched. But in spite of playing at Maine Road, City lost 2-0.

In the 1975 close season, Mike Summerbee left to play for Burnley, whilst Tony Book signed England international centre-half Dave Watson from Sunderland for 200,000. Though City's league form was inconsistent and ended the campaign in eighth place, the 1975-76 season was memorable for the club's performances in the League Cup. The Blues' first opponents were Norwich City but after a 1-1 draw at Carrow Road, the replay at Maine Road also ended all-square at 2-2 after extra-time. The third meeting at Stamford Bridge saw City run out winners 6-1 with Dennis Tueart grabbing a hat-trick. Goals from Bell and Royle helped City beat Nottingham Forest 2-1 and set up a fourth round derby match with Manchester United for the second year in succession. The Blues were in fine form and thrashed their rivals 4-0 with goals from Tueart (2) Hartford and Royle. Sadly, Colin Bell was injured in a tackle by Martin Buchan and was stretchered off. In the quarter-finals City beat Third Division Mansfield Town 4-2 to go through to the two-legged semi-final against Middlesbrough. The Blues lost the first-leg at Ayresome Park 1-0 but dominated the second game at Maine Road, winning 4-0 with goals from Keegan, Oakes, Barnes and Royle. The match against Newcastle United at Wembley was the club's third appearance in a final in seven years.

League Cup Final 1976
Manchester City 2 Newcastle United 1

The Magpies were suffering from injuries and a flu epidemic but could still field an England centre-forward, Malcolm Macdonald, to worry the Blues' defence. Newcastle dominated the opening minutes and Macdonald, forced Corrigan to palm his shot round the post. The Blues took the lead in the 11th minute when the PFA Young Player

McCLELLAND John B.
Bradford — 5 March 1935

Club				
Manchester City	03.53	8	0	2
Lincoln City	09.58	121	0	32
Queen's Park Rangers	09.61	71	0	23
Portsmouth	05.63	135	1	36
Newport County	07.68	36	0	10

McCORMACK Murdoch
Glasgow — 7 October 1920

Club				
Manchester City	04.47	1	0	0
Blackpool	07.47	12	0	3
Crewe Alexandra	07.48	31	0	3

McCOURT Frank J.
Portadown (NI) — 9 December 1925

Club				
Bristol Rovers	03.49	32	0	1
Manchester City	12.50	61	0	4
Colchester United	06.54	12	0	0

McDONALD Robert
Kilpatrick — 26 October 1935

Club				
Manchester City	09.56	5	0	0
Bournemouth	09.63	1	0	0

McDONALD Robert W.
Aberdeen — 13 April 1955

Club				
Aston Villa	09.72	33	6	3
Coventry City	08.76	161	0	14
Manchester City	10.80	96	0	11
Oxford United	09.83	93	1	14
Leeds United	02.87	18	0	1
Wolverhampton Wands (L)	02.88	6	0	0

McDOWALL Leslie J.
India — 25 October 1912

Club				
Sunderland	12.32	13	0	0
Manchester City	03.38	120	0	8
Wrexham	11.49	3	0	0

McGOLDRICK Edward J.
Islington — 30 April 1965

Club				
Northampton Town	08.86	97	10	9
Crystal Palace	01.89	139	8	11
Arsenal	06.93	32	6	0
Manchester City	09.96	39	1	0
Stockport County(L)	03.98	2	0	0

McILROY Samuel B.
Belfast — 2 August 1954

Club				
Manchester United	08.71	320	22	57
Stoke City	02.82	132	1	14
Manchester City	08.85	13	0	0
Bury	03.87	43	0	6

Asa Hartford

Asa Hartford was plucked from Scottish amateur football after being spotted by a West Bromwich Albion scout and signed professional forms for them in 1967, playing for them in the League Cup Final some three years later. He was soon thrilling the crowds with his skill and vision and it was only a matter of time before the inevitable big-money offer arrived to tempt Albion. Hartford will probably always be remembered as the player whose transfer to Leeds United was sensationally called off after a routine medical examination revealed a hole-in-the-heart condition. Showing great durability, the condition, happily for Asa, was a minor one and in August 1974 he joined Manchester City for £225,000. Making his debut in a 4-0 home win over West Ham United, he swept away all doubts about his fitness with his stamina and urgent play in midfield. He went on to play a major role in City's glorious era of the late 1970s, picking up a League Cup winners' medal with them in 1976.

In June 1979 he signed for Nottingham Forest under the management of Brian Clough for £500,000 but after only 63 days and three league games he was on his way back to the north-west with Everton. After two seasons and 98 appearances for the Merseysiders, Hartford moved back to Manchester City for £350,000 and a second spell. When City bought him for the second time, he was still a current Scottish international player. He won 50 Scottish caps, 36 of them in his two spells with the Blues. He played in 317 first team games for City before saying farewell to Maine Road in May 1984 to join Fort Lauderdale Sun in the NASL.

He later returned to First Division action with Norwich City and helped the Canaries win the 1985 League Cup when his shot was deflected by Sunderland's Chisholm for the only goal of the game. In July 1985 he joined Bolton Wanderers and was ever-present in his first season at Burnden Park, captaining the club to a Wembley appearance in the Freight Rover Trophy. He went on to join Stockport Coutny as player-manager before taking charge at Shrewsbury Town. He later coached at Blackburn and Stoke before being appointed assistant-manager at Maine Road in the summer of 1995, taking over from Alan Ball as caretaker boss 12 months later. Hartford is currently the Maine Road club's reserve team coach.

Bury	08.88	52	5	2
Preston North End	02.90	20	0	0

MacKENZIE Stephen
Romford 23 November 1961

Crystal Palace	07.79	0	0	0
Manchester City	07.79	56	2	8
West Bromwich Albion	08.81	153	3	23
Charlton Athletic	06.87	92	8	7
Sheffield Wednesday	02.91	51	0	2
Shrewsbury Town	12.91	24	0	1

McMAHON Stephen
Liverpool 20 August 1961

Everton	08.79	99	1	11
Aston Villa	05.83	74	1	7
Liverpool	09.85	202	2	29
Manchester City	12.91	83	4	1
SwindonTown	12.94	38	4	0

McMORRAN Edward J.
Larne (NI) 2 September 1923

Manchester City	08.47	33	0	12
Leeds United	01.49	38	0	6
Barnsley	07.50	104	0	30
Doncaster Rovers	02.53	126	0	32
Crewe Alexandra	11.57	24	0	6

McNAB Neil
Greenock 4 June 1957

Tottenham Hotspur	02.74	63	9	3
Bolton Wanderers	11.78	33	2	4
Brighton & Hove Albion	02.80	100	3	4
Leeds United	12.82	5	0	0
Manchester City	07.83	216	5	16
Tranmere Rovers	01.90	97	11	6
Huddersfield Town (L)	01.92	11	0	0

McNAUGHT Kenneth
Kirkaldy 11 January 1955

Everton	05.72	64	2	3
Aston Villa	08.77	207	0	8
WestBromwich Albion	08.83	42	0	1
Manchester City (L)	12.84	7	0	0
Sheffield United	07.85	34	0	5

MacRAE Keith
Glasgow 5 February 1951

Manchester City	10.73	56	0	0
Leeds United	03.82	0	0	0

McTAVISH John R.
Glasgow 2 February 1932

Manchester City	06.52	93	0	0

of the Year, Peter Barnes, fired home from close range following Joe Royle's knock-down. Newcastle equalised ten minutes from half-time when Gowling beat Corrigan and Watson to Macdonald's low centre to turn the ball into an empty net. There was no further scoring in the first-half but within a minute of the restart, Dennis Tueart had put City into the lead with a spectacular overhead kick. The north-east side had chances to equalise but as the game wore on, it was City who had the upper hand, though the score remained 2-1 at the final whistle. Tony Book had become the first man to win a major trophy as a player and as a manager.

In the summer of 1976, City lost the services of Alan Oakes, who after 680

Peter Barnes

The son of Ken Barnes, the City wing-half and chief scout, he joined the club straight from school and after turning professional in 1974, won England Youth honours.

He made his City debut in a 2-1 defeat at Burnley in October 1974, though

A Concise Post War History of Manchester City

it was midway through the following season before he won a regular place in the City side. His dazzling displays earned him Under-21 caps and in the League Cup Final of 1976, he scored in City's 2-1 win over Newcastle United. At the end of the season he was named as the Young Player of the Year.

In November 1977 he won the first of 22 caps for England when he played against Italy in a World Cup qualifier. An exciting winger, able to beat men with ease, he was surprisingly allowed to leave Maine Road and join West Bromwich Albion for a fee of £650,000 in 1979.

He ended his first season at the Hawthorns as the club's leading scorer with 15 goals and netted another 10 the following season before being sold to Leeds United for £930,000. Whilst at Elland Road he was loaned to Spanish Club Real Betis but in October 1984 was transferred to Coventry City after a brief loan spell with Manchester United. He spent a season at Highfield Road before joining United on a permanent basis.

In January 1987 he rejoined Manchester City but after taking his total of appearances to 161 in which he scored 22 goals he left to join Hull City after loan spells with Bolton Wanderers and Port Vale. He then jointed Bolton before later playing for a host of clubs including Sunderland, Stockport County and Wrexham and non-League clubs such as Northwich Victoria, Radcliffe Borough and Mossley. Barnes also had a spell as manager of Runcorn before resigning after two months.

MANN Arthur F.
Burntisland   23 January 1948

Manchester City	11.68	32	3	0
Blackpool (L)	11.71	3	0	0
NottsCounty	07.72	243	10	21
Shrewsbury Town	08.79	8	0	1
Mansfield Town	10.79	114	2	3

MARGETSON Martyn W.
Neath   8 September 1971

Manchester City	07.90	51	0	0
Bristol Rovers (L)	12.93	2	1	0
Southend United	08.98	32	0	0

MARSDEN Keith
Matlock   10 April 1934

Chesterfield	06.52	22	0	15
Manchester City	07.55	14	0	1
Accrington Stanley	08.59	0	0	0

MARSH Rodney W.
Hatfield   11 October 1944

Fulham	10.62	63	0	22
Queen's Park Rangers	03.66	211	0	106
Manchester City	03.72	116	2	36
Fulham	08.76	16	0	5

MASON Gary R.
Edinburgh   15 October 1979

Manchester City	10.96	18	1	0

MAY Andrew M.P.
Bury   26 January 1964

Manchester City	01.82	141	9	8
Huddersfield Town	07.87	112	2	5
Bolton Wanderers (L)	03.88	9	1	2
Bristol City	08.90	88	2	4
Millwall	08.92	52	2	1

MAZARELLI Giuseppe
Switzerland   14 August 1972

Manchester City (L)	03.96	0	2	0

MEADOWS James
Bolton   21 July 1931

Southport	03.49	6006		
Manchester City	03.51	130	0	30

MEGSON Gary J.
Manchester   2 May 1959

Plymouth Argyle	05.77	78	0	10
Everton	12.79	20	2	2
Sheffield Wednesday	08.81	123	0	13
NottinghamForest	08.84	0	0	0

The Blues

Dave Watson

A cornerstone of the England sides of the 1970s, Dave Watson played for Stapleford Old Boys before joining Notts County. Most of his games for the Meadow Lane club were at centre-forward but after moving to Rotherham United, Millers' manager Tommy Docherty switched him to centre-half. One of the best headers of a ball, he joined Sunderland in 1970, the first of a number of big money transfers. He made his international debut in 1974 by which time he had established himself as one of the best centre-halfs outside of the top flight and in 1976 he won an FA Cup winners' medal as Sunderland beat Leeds United. A big-hearted player he always seemed to have the strength to keep his balance and retain possession of the ball. He became an essential part of Ron Greenwood's England side and went on to win 65 caps. He kept him in the squad until the 1982 World Cup by which time he was 35.

Watson had joined Manchester City in the summer of 1975 and made his debut in a 3-0 win over Norwich City on the opening day of the 1975-76 season. He ended his first camapign at Maine Road with a League Cup winners' medal and in 1976-77 helped City to runners-up spot in the First Division. A virtual ever-present in his four seasons at Maine Road, he played briefly for Werder Bremen before returning to league action with Southampton whom he joined for £200,000. After two and a half seasons at The Dell he moved to Stoke City where he enjoyed an Indian summer. He was released to go on an 'illegal' tour to South Africa which never happened in the end but finally moved to Vancouver Whitecaps in the NASL. On his return he linked up with Derby County, later playing for Fort Lauderdale Sun, Notts County (again) and Kettering.

Newcastle United	11.84	21	3	1
Sheffield Wednesday	12.85	107	3	12
Manchester City	01.89	78	4	2
NorwichCity	08.92	42	4	1

MELLOR Ian
Sale	19 February 1950			
Manchester City	12.69	36	4	7
Norwich City	03.73	28	1	2
Brighton & Hove Albion	04.74	116	63	1
Chester City	02.78	38	2	11
Sheffield Wednesday	06.79	54	16	11
Bradford City	06.82	27	9	4

MELROSE James M.
Glasgow	7 October 1958			
Leicester City	07.80	57	15	21
Coventry City	09.82	21	3	8
Wolverhampton Wands	09.84	6	1	2
Manchester City	11.84	27	7	8
Charlton Athletic	03.86	44	4	19
Leeds United	09.87	3	1	0
Shrewsbury Town	02.88	27	22	3

MIKE Adrian R.
Manchester	16 November 1973			
Manchester City	07.92	2	0	1

MIMMS Robert A.
York	12 October 1963			
Halifax Town	08.81	0	0	0
Rotherham United	11.81	83	0	0
Everton	06.85	29	0	0
NottsCounty (L)	03.86	2	0	0
Sunderland (L)	12.86	4	0	0
Blackburn Rovers (L)	01.87	6	0	0
Manchester City (L)	09.87	3	0	0
Tottenham Hotspur	02.88	37	0	0
Blackburn Rovers	12.90	126	2	0
Crystal Palace	08.96	1	0	0
Preston North End	09.96	27	0	0
Rotherham United	08.97	43	0	0
York City	08.98	35	0	0

MORLEY David T.
St Helens	25 September 1977			
Manchester City	01.96	1	2	1
Southend United	08.98	26	1	0

MORLEY Trevor W.
Nottingham	20 March 1961			
Northampton Town	06.85	107	0	39
Manchester City	01.88	69	3	18
West Ham United	12.89	159	19	57
Reading	08.95	67	10	31

The Blues

first team appearances, joined Chester City for £15,000, but they did sign former United star Brian Kidd from Arsenal for £100,000. After drawing their first game of the 1976-77 season, 2-2 at Leicester City, the Blues were unbeaten for the first seven games and were in second place in the League, just a point behind Liverpool. City had already been knocked out of the League Cup by Aston Villa and had been drawn against Juventus in the UEFA Cup. Brian Kidd's first goal for the club gave them a 1-0 win over the Italian giants at Maine Road but it wasn't enough and the Blues went out in the first round after losing 2-0 in Turin. The club returned to league action and after picking up a point in a 2-2 draw at Everton at the beginning of October,

headed the table. The Blues only lost two of their first 25 matches and after losing 1-0 at Ipswich Town on 23 October were undefeated in 17 League and Cup games. Included in this sequence were FA Cup wins over West Bromwich Albion (Home 1-0 after a 1-1 draw) and Newcastle United (Away 3-1) before at the end of February they lost to a last-minute Trevor Cherry goal at Leeds United. Left with just the League to concentrate on, City maintained a top three place throughout the season. The title it seemed would go to either City, Liverpool or Ipswich. The Blues beat Ipswich at Maine Road at the beginning of April 2-1 with goals from Kidd and Watson but then on Easter Saturday travelled to Anfield to play Liverpool. City were a point behind the

A Concise Post War History of Manchester City

Kenny Clements

Kenny Clements made his league debut for Manchester City in a 1-0 defeat at Aston Villa in the fourth game of the 1975-76 season. He went on to appear in 27 games that season and also helped City reach the League Cup Final. However, towards the end of the season he had lost his place to Ged Keegan and missed out on City's 2-1 win over Newcastle in the Wembley final. Restored to the side for the start of the 1976-77 season, he helped the Blues to end the campaign as runners-up in Division One.

In September 1979, Clements was surprisingly transferred to Oldham Athletic for whom he made 206 league appearances in five and a half seasons at Boundary Park.

In March 1985 he returned to Maine Road for a second spell and the following month scored his only ever league goal for the Blues in a 2-0 home win over Sheffield United to help City win promotion to the First Division. Clements went on to appear in 282 League and Cup games before leaving Maine Road a second time to join Bury. He appeared in 81 league games for the Shakers before ending his league career with Shrewsbury Town.

MORRISON Andrew C.
Inverness · 30 July 1970

Plymouth Argyle	07.88	105	8	6
Blackburn Rovers	08.93	1	4	0
Blackpool	12.94	47	0	3
Huddersfield Town	07.96	43	2	2
Manchester City	10.98	21	1	4

MOULDEN Paul A.
Farnworth · 6 September 1967

Manchester City	09.84	48	16	18
Bournemouth	07.89	32	0	13
Oldham Athletic	03.90	17	21	4
Brighton & Hove Alb (L)	08.92	11	0	5
Birmingham City	03.93	18	2	5
Huddersfield Town	03.95	0	2	0
Rochdale	08.95	6	10	1

MULHEARN Kenneth J.
Liverpool · 16 October 1945

Everton	07.63	0	0	0
Stockport County	08.64	100	0	0
Manchester City	09.67	50	0	0
Shrewsbury Town	03.71	370	0	0
Crewe Alexandra	08.80	88	0	0

MUNDY James H.
Wythenshawe · 2 September 1948

Manchester City	08.66	2	1	0
Oldham Athletic	09.70	3	5	2

MUNRO James F.
Garmouth · 25 March 1926

Manchester City	11.47	25	0	4
Oldham Athletic	03.50	119	0	20
Lincoln City	02.53	161	0	24
Bury	01.58	41	0	8

MURRAY Hugh
Drybridge · 3 August 1936

Manchester City	04.55	1	0	0

MURRAY James R.
Dover · 11 October 1935

Wolverhampton Wands	11.53	273	0	155
Manchester City	11.63	70	0	43
Walsall	05.67	54	4	13

MURRAY William
Burnley · 26 January 1922

Manchester City	01.47	20	0	1

NIXON Eric.W.
Manchester · 4 October 1962

The Blues

Merseysiders and desperately needed to take at least a point from the game. Unfortunately Liverpool won 2-1 and went on to win the Championship with City in second place.

The top of the First Division table at the end of the 1976-77 season read:

	P.	W.	D.	L.	F.	A.	Pts
Liverpool	42	23	11	8	62	33	57
Manchester City	42	21	14	7	60	34	56
Ipswich Town	42	22	8	12	66	39	56

In the summer of 1977, City splashed out £300,000 on Southampton's Mick Channon and made a good start to the new campaign. Undefeated after four matches, the Blues were on top of the First Division when they met Manchester United in the Maine Road derby on 10 September 1977. The Reds too had made a good start but were soundly beaten 3-1 with Brian Kidd scoring twice against his former club and Mick Channon netting the Blues' other goal. City's next match was against Widzew Lodz of Poland in the UEFA Cup. Goals from Channon and Barnes gave the Blues a 2-0 lead but Polish international centre-forward Boniek scored two late goals. In the

Paul Power

Discovered by Harry Godwin, Manchester-born Paul Power was a student at Leeds Polytechnic when he was turning out for City's reserves in the Central League. He signed professional forms in the summer of 1975 and made his league debut at the same time as Kenny Clements in a 1-0 defeat at Aston Villa in the foiurth game of the 1975-76 season. Not a prolific goalscorer he opened his City account with the winner in a thrilling match against Derby County towards the end of the season, a game City won 4-3. In October 1979, Malcolm Allison handed Power the club captaincy and he celebrated by leading the Blues to a surprise 1-0 win over Nottingham Forest. The majority of Paul Power's career at Maine Road was spent on the left side of midfield though he was also played at left-back.

In 1981 he scored from a free-kick in the FA Cup semi-final defeat of Ipswich Town but couldn't repeat it in the Wembley final against Tottenham Hotspur. Power's second appearance at Wembley with City came in the 1986 Full Members' Cup Final when City lost 5-4 to Chelsea. Power's one and only representative honour came with an appearance in the England v Spain 'B' international.

He helped City win promotion to the top flight in 1984-85 but after one more season, after which he had taken his tally of goals to 36 in 445 first team games, Howard Kendall took him away from Maine Road and gave him a place in Everton's League Championship-winning side. Power later moved on to the coaching staff at Goodison Park but lost his job in November 1990 when Howard Kendall returned to the club. He joined the PFA as a community officer and is now their coaching secretary.

Manchester City	12.83	58	0	0
Wolverhampton Wands (L)	08.86	16	0	0
Bradford City (L)	11.86	3	0	0
Southampton (L)	12.86	4	0	0
Carlisle United (L)	01.87	16	0	0
Tranmere Rovers	03.88	341	0	0
Reading (L)	01.96	1	0	0
Blackpool (L)	02.96	20	0	0
Bradford City (L)	09.96	12	0	0
Stockport County	08.97	43	0	0
Wigan Athletic (L)	08.98	1	0	0
Wigan Athletic	03.99	2	0	0

OAKES Alan A.

Winsford	1 September 1942			
Manchester City	09.59	56	13	26
Chester City	07.76	211	0	15
Port Vale (N/C)	10.83	1	0	0

OAKES John

Hamilton	6 December 1919			
Huddersfield Town	11.43	0	0	0
Blackburn Rovers	02.47	35	0	9
Manchester City	06.48	77	0	9

OAKES Thomas

Manchester	6 February 1922			
Manchester City	04.47	1	0	0

OGDEN Trevor

Culcheth	12 June 1945			
Manchester City	09.64	9	0	3
Doncaster Rovers	06.65	38	0	14

OGLEY Alan

Barnsley	4 February 1946			
Barnsley	03.63	9	0	0
Manchester City	07.63	51	0	0
Stockport County	09.67	240	0	0
Darlington	08.75	80	0	0

OLDFIELD David C.

Australia	30 May 1968			
LutonTown	05.86	21	8	4
Manchester City	03.89	18	8	6
Leicester City	01.90	163	25	26
Millwall (L)	02.95	16	1	6
LutonTown	07.95	991	8	18
Stoke City	07.98	43	3	6

O'NEILL Martin H.M.

Kilrea (NI)	1 March 1952			
Nottingham Forest	10.71	264	21	48
Norwich City	02.81	11	0	1
Manchester City	06.81	12	1	0
Norwich City	01.82	54	1	11

The Blues

Ray Ranson

Right-back Ray Ranson joined Manchester City as an apprentice in the summer of 1976 and turned professional some twelve months later. He made his league debut for the Maine Road club in a goalless home draw against Nottingham Forest in December 1978 and was a virtual ever-present for the next five seasons. He left Maine Road in November 1984 to join Birmingham City for a fee of £15,000. However, after two seasons at St Andrew's he began to be troubled by a series of niggling injuries and struggled to regain full fitness. Once he had, however, he produced a number of outstanding performances which, after playing in 157 games, led to his move to Newcastle United. He made 102 appearances for the Magpies before returning to Maine Road and taking his total appearances in his two spells with the club to 235. He later ended his league career with Reading before becoming player-manager of non-League Witton Albion.

return leg, City failed to take their chances and the game ended goalless, the Polish side going through to the next round on the away goals rule. The result had an adverse effect on the club's league form and five defeats over the next couple of months saw them slip down the table. They bounced back with a 6-2 win over Chelsea with Dennis Tueart netting a hat-trick. The former Sunderland player scored another three goals on Boxing Day as City beat Newcastle United 4-0, a match in which Colin Bell made his comeback after two years out of the game. With Bell in the side, the Blues embarked on a nine-match unbeaten run and moved into third place. Dennis Tueart decided to leave Maine Road and signed for New York Cosmos for £250,000 - his transfer causing a lot of heartache among City supporters. Though the club kept up their challenge for the League title, too many of their remaining games ended in draws and they finished the season in fourth place, 12 points adrift of champions, Nottingham Forest.

During the summer of 1978, City spent a club record fee of £350,000 to bring England Under-21 international Paul Futcher to Maine Road. They followed it up by signing his twin brother Ron from Luton for 80,000. One player to leave the club was Mike Doyle, who after playing in 558 games, joined Stoke City.

The 1978-79 season saw City draw three of their first four matches before they recorded their first win, 3-0 over Norwich City. After beating Spurs 2-0, the Blues embarked on that season's UEFA Cup campaign and drew 1-1 with Twent Enschede in Holland before winning the return leg at Maine Road 3-2. In the next round, City played Standard Liege and beat the Belgian side 4-0 at Maine Road with three of the

NottsCounty	08.83	63	1	5

OWEN Gary A.

StHelens	7 July 1958			
Manchester City	08.75	101	2	19
West Bromwich Albion	06.79	185	2	21
Sheffield Wednesday	08.87	12	2	0

OWEN Robert

Farnworth	17 October 1947			
Bury	08.65	81	2	38
Manchester City	07.68	18	4	3
Swansea City (L)	03.70	5	1	1
Carlisle United	06.70	185	19	51
Northampton Town (L)	10.76	5	0	0
Workington (L)	12.76	8	0	2
Bury (L)	02.77	4	0	1
Doncaster Rovers	07.77	74	3	22

OXFORD Kenneth

Oldham	14 November 1929			
Manchester City	10.47	1	0	0
Chesterfield	06.50	0	0	0
Norwich City	07.51	128	0	0
DerbyCounty	12.57	151	0	0
Doncaster Rovers	07.64	16	0	0
Port Vale	03.65	0	0	0

PALMER Roger N.

Manchester	30 January 1959			
Manchester City	01.77	29	9	9
Oldham Athletic	11.80	419	47	141

PARDOE Glyn

Winsford	1 June 1946			
Manchester City	06.63	303	2	17

PARK Terence

Liverpool	7 February 1957			
Wolverhampton Wands	03.74	0	0	0
Stockport County	07.76	87	3	8
Stockport County	03.81	72	0	7
Manchester City (L)	01.83	0	2	0
Bury	07.83	18	3	1

PARLANE Derek J.

Helensburgh	5 May 1953			
Leeds United	03.80	45	5	10
Manchester City	08.83	47	1	20
Swansea City	01.85	21	0	3
Rochdale	12.86	42	0	10

PAUL Roy

TonPentre	19 April 1920			
Swansea City	10.38	160	0	14

club's goals coming in the final five minutes. In the second leg, Gary Owen was sent-off as City were beaten 2-0. Round three saw the Blues paired with Italian giants AC Milan. The first leg in the famous San Siro Stadium saw City race into a two-goal lead through Kidd and Power but the home side, who had three goals disallowed for offside, fought back to level the scores at 2-2. In fact, the Italians equalising goal came just eight minutes from time, preventing City from becoming the first British club ever to win in the San Siro. In the return leg at Maine Road, City ran out easy winners 3-0 with first-half goals from Booth, Hartford and Kidd. City were now through to the quarter-finals where they were drawn against Borussia Monchengladbech. The Blues were held to a 1 1 draw at Maine Road with the Germans' goal coming in the closing minutes of the match. Borussia won the second-leg 3-1 with City's goal scored by Kazimierz Deyna, the Polish international who had joined the club in November 1978.

The Blues, who had also been eliminated from the FA and League Cup competitions, were left with nothing to play for but pride and they ended the season in 15th place.

There was a mass exodus of players during the summer of 1979, with Gary Owen leading the way as he joined West Bromwich Albion for £450,000, a club record incoming transfer fee at the time. Others to leave Maine Road included Brian Kidd to Everton, Asa Hartford to Nottingham Forest and Peter Barnes to West Bromwich Albion. Also two matches into the 1979-80 season, Mick Channon returned to Southampton. It wasn't all one-way traffic and among the players to join the Blues were 17-year-old Steve MacKenzie from Crystal Palace for £250,000 - and he hadn't made his league debut yet ! The club also paid out £1. 4 million for Steve Daley from Wolves and £1. 2 million for Norwich City's Kevin Reeves. Sadly, this season in which Malcolm Allison was Team Manager and Tony Book the General Manager, Colin Bell announced his retirement. The new players took time to settle and after third round exits in both the FA and League Cups, City's season was one of a fight against relegation. One bright spot in the first half of the campaign was the Maine Road derby which saw the Blues beat United 2-0 with goals from Tony Henry and Mick Robinson, who had cost the club £750,000 from Preston North End. From Boxing Day 1979, the club went 17 games without a win, including losing the 100th Manchester derby at Old Trafford. Fortunately they won three of their last four games and ended the season in 17th place.

City made a disastrous start to the 1980-81 season when they failed to win any of their opening 12 league games. One of these matches was the Manchester derby at Old Trafford when, after going 2-1 down to a disputed Arthur Albiston goal, Roger Palmer equalised in the dying seconds of the game to secure a fully deserved point for the Blues. However, the next four games brought successive defeats and signalled the end for both Allison and Book. The new manager was Norwich City boss John Bond and though his first game in charge against Birmingham City was lost 1-0, he soon began to turn things around. He signed Tommy Hutchison and Bobby McDonald from Coventry City and Gerry Gow from Bristol City and between 15 November 1980 and 17 January 1981, City lost just one of 10 league matches. On 21 February, City entertained United in the local derby. A Steve MacKenzie goal clinched victory for the Blues in front of 50,114 spectators. Bond managed to keep the club out of the relegation zone and with City finishing the season in 12th place, it was their highest position for three seasons.

In the League Cup, Malcolm Allison's City had beaten Stoke City 4-1 on aggregate and Luton Town 2-1 before John Bond took charge of his first cup-tie against Notts County. Though he was unable to play any of his new signings, City ran out winners 5-1 with Dennis Tueart, who had returned to the fold, scoring four of the goals. In the fifth round, City came from behind to beat West Bromwich Albion 2-1 and set up a semi-final meeting with Liverpool. The first leg was held at Maine Road on 14 January 1981. In the opening minutes, Kevin Reeves had what looked a perfectly good goal disallowed for what the referee described as 'illegal jumping', a goal that would certainly have changed the course of the game. As it was, Ray Kennedy scored a late goal for Liverpool to give them a 1-0 victory to take back to Anfield. In the second leg, Dalglish scored to make it 2-0 on aggregate before Reeves pulled a goal back after Ray Clemence had failed to hold Steve MacKenzie's free-kick. Late in the game, Dave Bennett hit the bar for City but Liverpool hung on to win 2-1.

That season's FA Cup competition saw City reach the final for the eighth time in their history. In the third round the Blues were drawn at home to Malcolm Allison's Crystal Palace but though the former City boss received a tremendous welcome from the Maine Road fans, his side were emphatically beaten 4-0. The club's fourth round opponents were John Bond's former club, Norwich City.

Manchester City	07.50	270	0	9

PENNINGTON James
Golborne — 26 April 1939

Manchester City	08.56	1	0	0
Crewe Alexandra	03.61	34	0	2
Grimsby Town	04.63	89	0	8
Oldham Athletic	07.65	23	0	0
Rochdale	07.66	14	0	0

PERCIVAL John
Partington — 16 May 1913

Manchester City	10.32	161	0	8
Bournemouth	05.47	52	0	1

PHELAN Terence M.
Manchester — 16 March 1967

Leeds United	08.84	12	2	0
Swansea City	07.86	45	0	0
Wimbledon	07.87	155	4	1
Manchester City	08.92	102	1	2
Chelsea	11.95	13	2	0
Everton	01.97	23	1	0

PHILLIPS David O.
Wegburg,Germany — 29 July 1963

Plymouth Argyle	08.81	65	8	15
Manchester City	08.84	81	0	13
Coventry City	06.86	93	7	8
Norwich City	07.89	152	0	18
Nottingham Forest	08.93	116	10	5
Huddersfield Town	11.97	44	8	3
Lincoln City	03.99	9	0	0

PHILLIPS Ernest
North Shields — 29 November 1923

Manchester City	01.47	80	0	0
Hull City	11.51	42	0	0
York City	06.54	164	0	2

PHILLIPS Martin
Exeter — 13 March 1976

Exeter City	07.94	36	16	5
Manchester City	11.95	3	12	0
ScunthorpeUtd (L)	01.98	2	1	0
Exeter City (L)	03.98	7	1	0
Portsmouth	08.98	2	15	1
Bristol Rovers (L)	02.99	2	0	0

PHOENIX Ronald J.
Stretford — 30 June 1929

Manchester City	03.50	53	0	2
Rochdale	02.60	64	0	0

The Blues

Nicky Reid

Hailing from Davyhulme, Nicky Reid arrived at Maine Road from Whitehall Juniors and after working his way through the ranks, was given his first team debut in the UEFA Cup match against Borussia Moenchengladbach at Maine Road which ended all-square at 1-1. Later the hard-running midfielder made his league debut in a 2-1 defeat at Ipswich Town. Apart from a short spell with Seattle Sounders in the NASL, Nicky Reid was a virtual ever-present in the City side for seven seasons until his transfer to Blackburn Rovers on a free transfer in the summer of 1987.

Capped six times by England at Under-21 level, Reid gave the Ewood Park club great service, appearing in 209 games before following a loan spell with Bristol City, he signed for West Bromwich Albion in November 1992. After a short spell at the Hawthorns, he joined Wycombe Wanderers before playing non-League football with Woking and later Witton Albion. In December 1995 he returned to league action with Bury where he showed his versatility before being released after two seasons with the Shakers.

After former Carrow Road star Kevin Reeves had opened the scoring in the 16th minute, goals from Gow, MacKenzie, Bennett, Power and McDonald gave the Blues a 6-0 win and a place in round five against Fourth Division Peterborough United. City travelled to London Road for what appeared on paper a foregone conclusion. 'The Posh' had their chances to create an upset but the game's only goal was scored by Tommy Booth, who had been selected in place of the young Tommy Caton. In the quarter-finals, City played Everton at

PLENDERLEITH John B.
Bellshill	6 October 1937			
Manchester City	07.60	41	0	0

POINTON Neil G.
Warsop	28 November1964			
Scunthorpe United	08.82	159	0	2
Everton	11.85	95	7	5
Manchester City	07.90	74	0	2
Oldham Athletic	07.92	92	3	3
Walsall	07.98	43	0	0

POLLOCK Jamie
Stockton	16 February 1974			
Middlesbrough	12.91	144	11	17
Bolton Wanderers	11.96	43	3	5
Manchester City	03.98	32	2	2

POWELL Ronald W.H.
Knighton	2 December 1929			
Manchester City	11.48	12	0	0
Chesterfield	06.52	471	0	0

POWER Paul C.
Manchester	30 October 1953			
Manchester City	09.73	358	7	26
Everton	06.86	52	2	6

PRITCHARD Harvey J.
Meriden	30 January 1918			
Coventry City	10.35	5	0	2
Crystal Palace	06.37	30	0	6
Manchester City	03.38	22	0	5
Southend United	02.47	72	0	8

QUIGLEY Michael A.
Manchester	2 October 1970			
Manchester City	07.89	3	9	0
Wrexham (L)	02.95	4	0	0
Hull City	07.95	3	4	1

QUINN Niall J.
Dublin	6 October 1966			
Arsenal	11.83	59	8	14
Manchester City	03.90	183	20	66
Sunderland	08.96	77	9	34

RANSON Raymond
St Helens	12 June 1960			
Manchester City	06.77	181	2	1
Birmingham City	11.84	136	1	0
Newcastle United	12.88	78	5	1
Manchester City	08.92	17	0	0
Reading	08.93	22	2	0

The Blues

Tommy Caton

Tommy Caton was captain of England Schoolboys at centre-half when joining Manchester City as an apprentice during the summer of 1978. In his first season at Maine Road he helped the Blues to the FA Youth Cup Final where they were beaten by Millwall. In August 1979 he made his league debut for City as a 16-year-old apprentice in a goalless home draw against Crystal Palace and during the campaign he became the youngest player in the history of the Football League to remain ever-present in a season. Caton also won five England Youth caps and was still eligible to play in the 1980 FA Youth Cup Final against Aston Villa. Over the next two seasons, Tommy Caton was the backbone of the City defence and was a member of the side that lost to Spurs in the 1981 FA Cup Final. His performances earned him nine Under-21 caps and when he played against Arsenal at Maine Road in March 1982 he became the youngest player in the history of the Football League to reach the milestone of 100 First Division games. However, when City were relegated to the Second Division in 1982-83, Caton was transferred to Arsenal for £500,000.

After a couple of seasons at Highbury, he was facing stiff competition from David O'Leary, Martin Keown and the fast emerging Tony Adams and so in January 1987 he moved to Oxford United. After less than 18 months at the Manor Ground he joined Charlton Athletic. Sadly at the end of the 1991-92 season he was forced to retire from the game when a long-term injury resuurected itself.

In April 1993 the footballing public were shocked and stunned when hearing of the tragic and untimely death of Tommy Caton, aged 30.

A Concise Post War History of Manchester City

Goodison Park. They fell behind to a Peter Eastoe goal three minutes before the interval but equalised on the stroke of half-time when Gerry Gow crashed home Kevin Reeves' lay-off. The second-half was only three minutes old when Caton wrestled Varadi to the ground for a blatant penalty which was converted by Trevor Ross. City pushed forward and were rewarded for their endeavbours when captain Paul Power levelled the scores in the 84th minute. In the Maine Road replay, two goals from Bobby McDonald and another from Power gave City a 3-1 win. The Blues' semi-final opponents were Ipswich Town who were hopeful of winning the 'treble'. After·90 minutes the game was goalless but a goal in extra-time by Paul Power took City into the final.

City's opponents in what was the 100th FA Cup FInal were Tottenam Hotspur. The Maine Road club dominated the early exchanges, forcing four corners in as many minutes. It came as no surprise when after 29 minutes they took the lead as Tommy Hutchison dived to head home a Ray Ranson centre. The Blues almost extended their lead 13 minutes into the second-half when Steve MacKenzie's shot hit Aleksic's right-hand post. There were just ten minutes left to play when Spurs were awarded a free-kick some 20 yards out following Gerry Gow's foul on Ardilles. The little Argentinian rolled the ball to Hoddle who curled his shot round the City wall where it hit Hutchison on the shoulder and deflected past Corrigan for the equaliser. There was no further scoring in extra-time and so the two sides met again five days later in front of a Wembley crowd of 92,500. They were treated to two early goals as Villa put Spurs ahead after seven minutes only

REDMOND Stephen

Liverpool   2 November1967

Manchester City	12.84	231	4	7
Oldham Athletic	07.92	195	10	4
Bury	07.98	26	0	0

REEVES Kevin P.

Burley   20 October 1957

Bournemouth	07.75	60	3	20
Norwich City	01.77	118	1	37
Manchester City	03.80	129	1	34
Burnley	07.83	20	1	12

REID Nicholas S.

Urmston   30 October 1960

Manchester City	10.78	211	5	2
Blackburn Rovers	07.87	160	14	9
Bristol City (L)	09.92	3	1	0
West Bromwich Albion	11.92	13	7	0
Wycombe Wanderers	03.94	6	2	0
Bury	12.95	19	6	0

REID Peter

Huyon   20 June1956

Bolton Wanderers	05.74	222	3	23
Everton	12.82	155	4	8
Queen's Park Rangers	02.89	29	0	1
Manchester City	12.89	90	13	1

REVIE Donald G.

Middlesbrough   10 July 1927

Leicester City	08.44	96	0	25
Hull City	11.49	76	0	12
Manchester City	10.51	162	0	37
Sunderland	11.56	64	0	15
Leeds United	12.58	77	0	11

RIGBY John

Golborne   29 July 1924

Manchester City	12.46	100	0	0

ROBINS Mark G.

AshtonunderLyne   22 December 1969

Manchester United	12.86	19	29	11
Norwich City	08.92	57	10	20
Leicester City	01.95	40	16	12
Reading (L)	08.97	5	0	0
Manchester City	03.99	0	2	0

ROBINSON Michael J.

Leicester   12 July 1958

Preston North End	07.76	45	3	15
Manchester City	07.79	29	1	8
Brighton & Hove Albion	07.80	111	2	37

The Blues

for City to equalise three minutes later with a devastating 20-yard volley by Steve MacKenzie. Five minutes into the second-half, City took the lead when Miller was adjudged to have pushed Bennett and Kevin Reeves converted the resultant penalty. A 70th minute leveller by Crooks made it 2-2 and five minutes later Ricky Villa scored a magnificent goal, weaving his way through the City defence before placing the ball through Joe Corrigan's legs. Dennis Tueart replaced Bobby

McDonald and he came close to taking the tie into extra-time, but it wasn't to be and the trophy went to the White Hart Lane club.

During the close season John Bond went back to his former club Norwich City to sign Northern Ireland international Martin O'Neill and after just two gams of the 1981-82 season splashed out £1. 2 million to bring Nottingham Forest's Trevor Francis to Maine Road. He made his debut at Stoke City and scored twice in a 3-1

Neil McNab

Neil McNab was only 15 years old when he played for Morton in the Scottish First Division, signing for Spurs for £40,000 in February 1974. A hard-working gritty midfield player, it took him until 1977-78 to establish a place in the White Hart Lane club's first team. He was ever-present in the club's Second Division promotion campaign and won Scottish Under-21 honours to add to his schoolboy and youth honours. After losing his place in a Spurs midfield of Ardilles, Hoddle and Villa, he joined Bolton Wanderers for £250,000. He then moved around playing for Brighton, Leeds United on loan, and Portsmouth on loan before a permanent move to Manchester City. He made his debut for the Blues in a 2-0 win at Crystal Palace on the opening day of the 1983-84 season. He missed very few games over the next six seasons, being ever-present in 1986-87. He proved invaluable in helping the club win promotion for a second time during his stay at Maine Road in 1988-89 but in December 1989 he was sold to Tranmere Rovers.

At the end of his first season at Prenton Park, he had helped Rovers win the Leyland Daf Cup and reach the play-offs where they lost in the final to Notts County. In 1991 the club won promotion to the Second Division though McNab missed the play-off final win over Bolton Wanderers. He went on to score eight goals in 139 games before leaving to join Ayr United.

Liverpool	08.83	26	4	6
Queen's Park Rangers	12.84	41	7	6

ROBINSON Peter

Manchester	29 January 1922			
Manchester City	05.40	100		
Chesterfield	10.47	6000		
NottsCounty	02.50	8201		

ROCASTLE David C.

Lewisham	2 May 1967			
Arsenal	12.84	204	14	24
Leeds United	08.92	17	8	2
Manchester City	12.93	21	0	2
Chelsea	08.94	27	2	0
Norwich City (L)	01.97	11	0	0
Hull City (L)	10.97	10	0	1

RODGER Simon L.

Shoreham	3 October 1971			
Crystal Palace	07.90	151	22	8
Manchester City (L)	10.96	8	0	1
Stoke City (L)	02.97	5	0	0

ROSLER Uwe

Attenburg,Germany	15 November 1968			
Manchester City	03.94	141	11	50

ROYLE Joseph

Liverpool	9 April 1949			
Everton	08.66	229	3	102
Manchester City	12.74	98	1	23
Bristol City	11.77	100	1	18
Norwich City	08.80	40	2	5

RUDD James J.

Dublin	25 October 1919			
Manchester City	01.38	2	0	0
York City	03.47	83	0	23
Leeds United	02.49	18	0	1
Rotherham United	10.49	75	0	10
Scunthorpe United	10.51	32	0	5
Workington	09.52	17	0	1

RUSSELL Craig S.

South Shields	4 February 1974			
Sunderland	07.92	103	47	31
Manchester City	11.97	22	9	2
Tranmere Rovers (L)	08.98	3	0	10
Port Vale (L)	01.99	8	0	1

RYAN John G.

Lewisham	20 July 1947			
Fulham	07.65	42	5	1
LutonTown	07.69	264	2	10

win for the Blues. That season also saw the arrival of the manager's son Kevin Bond and the return of the much-loved Asa Hartford. The club's form up until the turn of the year was good and at New Year, the Blues were top of the table, although a couple of clubs had games in hand. Sadly results fell away and City ended the season in 10th place. The two Cup competitions saw City eliminated in the fourth round, losing 3-1 at Coventry in the FA Cup, and 1-0 at Barnsley in the League Cup. The second round League Cup tie against Stoke City had ended all-square at 2-2 after both teams had won their home leg 2-0 and resulted in it becoming the first domestic game in England to be decided by penalties.

City made a good start to the 1982-83 campaign, winning their first three matches to go top of the table, although

A Concise Post War History of Manchester City

Steve Redmond

Although born on Merseyside, Steve Redmond joined Manchester City as an associated schoolboy player before becoming an apprentice in the summer of 1984. Even after turning professional, he had to wait over 12 months for a chance of first team action. Whilst he was learning his trade, he was captaining the City youth team to victory over Manchester United in the FA Youth Cup Final of 1986.

By then he had already made his league debut in a 2-0 home win over Queen's Park Rangers. He soon began to hold down a regular place and was ever-present in 1987-88 when the fans named him 'Player of the Year'.

As club captain he led the team back to the First Division as runners-up in 1988-89. A run of 138 consecutive league games was halted by injury at the start of the 1990-91 season but he soon returned to lend his experience to a young City side. After playing in all but one of the first 30 games of the 1991-92 season, he was suddenly dropped, first in favour of David Brightwell and then Michel Vonk. In the summer of 1992 he moved to Oldham Athletic along with Neil Pointon plus £300,000 as Rick Holden travelled in the opposite direction. He went on to play in 239 games for the Latics before being allowed to join Bury on a free transfer in July 1998.

Norwich City	08.76	113	3	26
Sheffield United	09.80	56	0	2
Manchester City	01.82	19	0	0
Stockport County (N/C)	08.83	1	1	0
Chester (N/C)	09.83	4	0	0
CambridgeUnited (N/C)	10.84	5	0	0

SAMBROOK Raymond
Wolverhampton   31 May 1933

Coventry City	09.53	96	0	25
Manchester City	01.58	62	0	13
Doncaster Rovers	06.62	8	0	0
Crewe Alexandra	01.63	0	0	0

SAVAGE John A.
Bromley   14 December 1929

Hull City	09.50	4	0	0
Halifax Town	03.52	57	0	1
Manchester City	11.53	30	0	0
Walsall	01.58	51	0	0

SCOTT Ian
Radcliffe   20 September 1967

Manchester City	09.85	20	4	3
Stoke City	07.89	21	9	2
Crewe Alexandra (L)	03.91	12	0	1

SCULLY Anthony D.T.
Dublin   12 June 1976

Crystal Palace	12.93	0	3	0
Bournemouth (L)	10.94	6	4	0
CardiffCity (L)	01.96	13	1	0
Manchester City	08.97	1	8	0
Stoke City (L)	01.98	7	0	0
Queen's Park Rangers	03.98	17	13	2

SEAGRAVES Mark
Bootle   22 October 1966

Liverpool	11.83	0	0	0
Norwich City (L)	11.86	3	0	0
Manchester City	09.87	36	6	0
Bolton Wanderers	09.90	152	5	7
SwindonTown	06.95	57	4	0

SEAR Clifford R.
Rhostyllen   22 September 1936

Manchester City	01.57	248	0	1
Chester City	04.68	49	2	1

SHAWCROSS David F.
Stretford   3 July 1941

Manchester City	06.58	47	0	2
Stockport County	06.65	59	1	14
Halifax Town	03.67	126	6	17

The Blues

Ian Brightwell

Son of the famous Olympic athletes, Ann Packer and Robbie Brightwell, Ian has a younger brother David, who also began his career at Maine Road. He won an FA Youth Cup winners' medal before he made his league debut in a 3-1 win over Wimbledon on the opening day of the 1986-87 season. Initially a midfielder, he was surprisingly discarded midway through the successful 1988-89 promotion campaign in favour of new signing Gary Megson. In 1990-91 he was given a new role at right-back at least until the arrival of Andy Hill from Bury. An infrequent scorer, his equalising goal - a rasping 35-yard drive against United in the Manchester 'derby' game in February 1990 - endeared him to the hearts of City fans forever! Although he later re-established himself in midfield, he was used more as a utility player. Sadly over the following seasons, injuries hampered his progress though he still managed to fit into the plans of the various managers who have been in charge of the club. He went on to appear in 382 games before joining Coventry City in June 1998.

Again injuries limited his first team opportunities to just one and in the summer of 1999 he was released by the Highfield Road club.

the 1-0 win over newly promoted Watford resulted in Joe Corrigan dislocating his shoulder. Though Bobby McDonald donned the 'keepers' jersey and performed heroics as the Hornets did all the attacking, Corrigan's eventual replacement was Alex Williams, the first black goalkeeper in the First Division. Though he proved to be one of the club's most consistent performers, results were mixed both in the League and the newly named Milk Cup where, after beating Wigan Athletic over two legs, City lost to Southampton after a replay. In the FA Cup, City beat Sunderland 2-1 after the first game at Roker Park had ended goalless but were then well beaten by Brighton and Hove Albion 4-0. This was followed

almost immediately by John Bond's resignation. His assistant John Benson was appointed manager but after losing 11 of their next 16 matches, City found themselves needing a point from their last game against Luton Town to ensure survival. The first-half was goalless but with City content to sit back and defend it was the Hatters who came closest to scoring when Kirk Stephens rattled the bar with Williams beaten. There were just four minutes left when Luton substitute Raddy Antic's shot was deflected past Williams for what proved to be the game's only goal - City were down and the following season would be playing Second Division football for the first time since 1965-66.

The close season saw John Benson

replaced by former Aberdeen and Celtic manager Billy McNeill, whilst on the playing side, Dennis Tueart joined Stoke City and Joe Corrigan left to play for Seattle Sounders after 17 years at Maine Road. McNeill brought in Parlane, Tolmie and McNab and the three Scots helped City make a good start to the 1983-84 season. Following five successive victories in September and October, the Blues moved into second place behind Sheffield Wednesday and though results over the next few months were mixed, City remained in contention for one of the three promotion places. Chelsea and Sheffield Wednesday seemed assured of finishing in the top two places, whilst third place rested between City and Newcastle United. Kevin Keegan had helped the Magpies to beat City 5-0 earlier in the season and scored the all-important second goal for the Geordies when they won 2-1 at Maine Road in February. That result left the sides level on points but with Newcastle having a game in hand. Results over Easter went against the club and after losing 2-0 at home to Chelsea in what was the first-ever Second Division game to be shown live on television, the Blues hopes of an immediate return to the top flight had gone. City beat already relegated Cambridge United 5-0 in the final game of the season to finish fourth, ten points adrift of third-placed Newcastle, while Sheffield Wednesday were runners-up to champions, Chelsea.

City began the 1984-85 season as one of the promotion favourites but there was little cause for excitement in the first half of the camapign after a series of indifferent results. After the turn of the year, City began to climb up the table and in March after beating Blackburn Rovers 1-0 at Ewood Park, courtesy of a Steve Kinsey goal, actually

SHELIA Murtaz
Tbilisi, Georgia	25 March 1969			
Manchester City	11.97	15	0	2

SHERON Michael N.
Liverpool	11 January 1972			
Manchester City	07.90	82	18	24
Bury (L)	03.91	1	4	1
Norwich City	08.94	19	9	2
Stoke City	11.95	64	5	34
Queen's Park Rangers	07.97	57	6	19
Barnsley	01.99	14	1	2

SHINTON Robert T.
WestBromwich	6 January 1952			
Walsall	03.72	78	1	20
Cambridge United	03.74	99	025	
Wrexham	07.76	128	0	37
Manchester City	07.79	5	0	0
Millwall (L)	02.80	5	0	3
Newcastle United	03.80	41	1	10
Millwall	03.82	29	5	4

SHUTT Carl S.
Sheffield	10 October 1961			
Sheffield Wednesday	05.85	36	4	16
Bristol City	10.87	39	7	10
Leeds United	03.89	46	33	17
Birmingham City	08.93	18	8	4
Manchester City (L)	12.93	5	1	0
Bradford City	08.94	60	28	15
Darlington	03.97	28	2	59

SILKMAN Barry
Stepney	29 June 1952			
Hereford United	08.74	18	19	2
Crystal Palace	08.76	40	8	6
Plymouth Argyle	10.78	14	0	2
LutonTown (L)	02.79	300		
Manchester City	03.79	19	0	3
Brentford	08.80	14	0	1
Queen's Park Rangers	10.80	22	1	2
Leyton Orient	09.81	133	7	14
Southend United	07.85	38	2	1
Crewe Alexandra (N/C)	09.86	1	1	0

SIMPSON Fitzroy
Bradfordon, sAvon	26 February 1970			
SwindonTown	07.88	78	2	79
Manchester City	03.92	58	13	4
Bristol City (L)	09.94	4	0	0
Portsmouth	08.95	122	9	10

The Blues

David White

Discovered on the club's doorstep, David White made his debut as a substitute in a 1-0 defeat at Luton Town in September 1986. He did well enough to hold down a place on the right-wing for short spells although the club sank into the Second Division at the end of the season. White sprang to fame in 1987-88 in a City team brimming with brilliant youngsters and scored a hat-trick in the 10-1 demolition of Huddersfield Town. Promotion was achieved the following season with White playing in all but one game as he did in 1989-90 when City struggled to hold on to their First Division status. Always noted for his confident surging runs and powerful shooting, he was switched from the wing to central striker by manager Peter Reid in January 1990 following the signing of Mark Ward. It was an inspired move as he formed a prolific goalscoring partnership with Niall Quinn, his 16 goals including four in a 5-1 win at Aston Villa. He was the club's top scorer in 1991-92 when his total of 19 goals included his third hat-trick for the club in a 5-2 win at Oldham Athletic. He was ever-present in 1992-93 when he also made his full England debut against Spain at Satander. He went on to score 96 goals in 342 League and Cup games before joining Leeds United in December 1993 for a fee of £2 million.

Sadly he struggled with injury and the burden of replacing Gordon Strachan. He never held down a regular place because of ankle trouble and in January 1996 he was sold to Sheffield United for £500,000.

Again a series of niggling injuries and an operation with a long recovery rate had limited his first team appearances for the Blades.

went to the top of the Second Division. However, the Blues had played more games than their main challengers, Oxford United, Portsmouth and Birmingham City. On 23 March 1985, City travelled to the Manor Ground but were well beaten 3-0 by Oxford. This setback was followed by two draws and a defeat which left the club in fifth place. Victories over Sheffield United and Portsmouth lifted the Blues back into the top three but only a draw against Oldham and a 3-2 defeat at

Notts County, left City needing to beat Charlton Athletic at Maine Road in the final game of the season. A crowd of 47,285 saw goals from Phillips (2) May, Melrose and Simpson help City to beat the Addicks 5-1 and thus win promotion for the Maine Road club.

The 1985-86 season saw City struggle to acclimatise to top flight football, winning just two of their opening 16 league games. These victories were both in August as West Bromwich Albion were beaten 3-2 and Tottenham

Hotspur 2-1. The club then had to wait until the middle of November for their next victory when Nottingham Forest were defeated 2-0. Before the turn of the year, City had beaten Coventry City 5-1 and Liverpool 1-0 in front of a Boxing Day crowd of 35,584. During the second half of the season, the club's league form was indifferent and they had to settle for 15th place in a campaign in which consolidation was their main aim. Despite poor performances in both the FA and League Cup, City did reach Wembley in the Full Members' Cup, a competition created for teams in the top two divisions not involved in the 'Super Cup'. City won both their group games, beating Leeds United 6-1 and Sheffield United 2-1, to qualify for the Northern Area semi-final against Sunderland. The match ended goalless but City won 4-3 on penalties. The two-legged Northern Area final saw City lose 2-1 at Hull City but in the second leg, goals from Phillips and Melrose gave the Blues victory 3-2 on aggregate.

The final against Chelsea was most entertaining. Steve Kinsey had given City an eighth minute lead but goals from Speedie and Lee gave Chelsea a 2-1 half-time lead. City were denied a penalty within minutes of the resumption and then almost immediately Speedie broke away to extend the Londoner's lead. The much-travelled forward completed his hat-trick in the 58th minute and when Colin Lee netted his second, Chelsea led 5-1 with just over ten minutes to play. Mark Lillis pulled a goal back before Doug Rougvie headed past his own 'keeper and when Andy May was tripped in the area, Lillis scored from the spot to make it 5-4. It was an amazing fight back by City and if there had been another ten minutes to play, City would most certainly have

SIMPSON Paul D.
Carlisle   26 July 1966

Manchester City	08.83	99	22	18
Oxford United	10.88	138	6	43
DerbyCounty	02.92	134	52	48
Sheffield United (L)	12.96	2	4	0
Wolverhampton Wands	10.97	31	8	6
Walsall (L)	09.98	4	0	1
Walsall (L)	12.98	6	0	0

SINCLAIR Graeme
Paisley   1 July 1957

Manchester City	11.84	1	0	0

SMITH Frederick E.
Draycott   7 May 1926

Derby County	06.47	1	0	0
Sheffield United	03.48	53	0	17
Manchester City	05.52	2	0	1
Grimsby Town	09.52	50	0	24
Bradford City	07.54	9	0	3

SMITH George B.
Fleetwood   7 February 1921

Manchester City	05.38	166	0	75
Chesterfield	10.51	250	0	97

SMITH Gordon D.
Kilwinning   29 December 1954

Brighton & Hove Albion	06.80	97	12	22
Manchester City	03.84	40	2	13
Oldham Athletic	01.86	14	1	0

SOWDEN William
Manchester   8 December 1930

Manchester City	04.49	11	0	2
Chesterfield	11.54	97	0	59
Stockport County	06.57	15	0	7

SPROSTON Bert
Sandbach   22 June 1915

Leeds United	06.33	130	0	1
Tottenham Hotspur	06.38	9	0	0
Manchester City	11.38	125	0	5

SPURDLE William
Guernsey   28 January 1926

Oldham Athletic	03.48	56	0	5
Manchester City	01.50	160	0	32
Port Vale	11.56	21	0	7
Oldham Athletic	06.57	144	0	19

STEPANOVIC Dragoslav
Yugoslavia   30 August 1948

The Blues

gone on to win the trophy ! The 1985-86 season also saw the Blues win the FA Youth Cup, beating Manchester United 3-1 on aggregate in the final.

During the close season, Paul Power left Maine Road to join Everton after appearing in 445 games for City. The 1986-87 season was only seven games old when Billy McNeill left the club to manage Aston Villa and was replaced by his assistant Jimmy Frizzell. He was soon active in the transfer market, bringing in Imre Varadi, Tony Grealish and John Gidman. However, when City met United in the first Manchester derby of the season at the end of October, the Blues were bottom of the First Division. A Mick McCarthy goal gave City a 1-1 draw which was followed by a draw and two victories, including a 3-1 win over Billy McNeill's Aton Villa. Sadly the Blues fell away again and a number of disappointing defeats left them fighting relegation. This was finally confirmed on 9 May 1987 when the Blues lost 2-0 at West Ham United. In the Cup competitions, City lost 1-0 to Manchester United in the FA Cup and 3-1 to Arsenal in the League Cup to complete a thoroughly miserable season for the Maine Road club.

In the summer, Norwich City coach Mel Machin was appointed Team Manager whilst Jimmy Frizzell moved to the General Manager's post. City were lying in mid-table when on 7 November 1987, Huddersfield Town visited Maine Road for what proved to be one of the most remarkable matches in the club's history. Despite the Yorkshire club's early pressure it was Neil McNab who opened the scoring, putting City ahead in the 12th minute. This goal led to City dominating the rest of the first-half and strikes from Stewart, Adcock and White put them 4-

0 up at half-time. The second-half was only seven minutes old when Tony Adcock, who had joined the club from Colchester United in the close season, made it 5-0. Paul Stewart made it six in the 66th minute and within a matter of seconds, Adcock had completed his hat-trick to put the Blues 7-0 up. Ten minutes from time, Paul Stewart completed his hat-trick and in the 85th minute, David White made it nine. Two minutes from time, former City favourite Andy May scored from the penalty-spot before David White completed his hat-trick to make the final score 10-1. Three players had scored hat-tricks in what was the club's best score at Maine Road. Three days later Tony Adcock scored another hat-trick in a 6-2 Simod Cup win over Plymouth Argyle but the club's league form left a lot to be dsired. Just before Christmas the Blues were in fifth place but results after the turn of the year saw them return to a mid-table position. The club were still hopeful of winning a play-off place but had to settle for ninth place at the end of the season.

In the two major Cup competitions, City proved they could still deliver the goods when they played to their full potential. In the League Cup, Wolves were beaten 3-2 on aggregate before First Division Nottingham Forest were defeated 3-0. Another top flight club in Watford were beaten 3-1 in round four before the Blues lost 2-0 at Everton. In the FA Cup, City faced Huddersfield Town in the third round at Leeds Road. The Yorkshire side were determined to avenge the 10-1 defeat earlier in the season and led 2-1 with just seconds remaining. City were awarded a free-kick just outside the penalty area and John Gidman curled the ball round the wall and in off the post to force a replay. City were the better team in the Maine Road game three days later but couldn't beat Huddersfield 'keeper Brian Cox, even after extra-time, and the game remained goalless. The second replay at Leeds Road saw City at last have some luck in front of goal, winning 3-0 to earn a fourth round tie at Blackpool. The Seasiders took the lead in the 82nd minute but City, who had outplayed the home side for much of the match, kept pushing forward and scored a deserved equaliser in injury-time, courtesy of Paul Lake. In the replay, goals from Stewart and Simpson helped the Blues to a 2-1 win.

Plymouth Argyle were City's opponents in round five but the Maine Road club were the better side on the day and ran out winners 3-1. City were in the quarter-finals for the first time since 1981 but their opponents were Liverpool who were already running away with the League Championship. Though City had the better of the early exchanges and came close to scoring on a couple of occasions, the Merseyside outfit proved too strong and went on to win 4-0.

Promotion was obviously the main priority of the 1988-89 season but after a 1-0 defeat at Hull City on the opening day of the season and a 4-1 beating by Oldham Athletic at Maine Road two days later, it wasn't the greatest of starts. After a couple of draws, City won their first game of the season, beating Brighton and Hove Albion 2-1. Victories at Chelsea and Barnsley followed before a Wayne Biggins goal was enough to beat League leaders Blackburn Rovers. Despite a couple of 1-0 defeats at Ipswich and West Bromwich Albion, by the time City had beaten Bradford City 4-0 on 10 December, they were top of the league. As the club continued to battle for promotion, large inflatable

Manchester City	08.79	14	1	0

STEWART Paul A.
Manchester	7 October 1964			
Blackpool	10.81	188	13	56
Manchester City	03.87	51	0	26
Tottenham Hotspur	06.88	126	5	28
Liverpool	07.92	28	4	1
Crystal Palace (L)	01.94	18	0	3
Wolverhampton Wands (L)	09.94	5	3	2
Burnley (L)	02.95	6	0	0
Sunderland (L)	08.95	1	1	0
Sunderland	03.96	30	4	5
Stoke City	06.97	2	0	3

STOBART Barry H.
Doncaster	6 June 1938			
Wolverhampton Wands	12.55	49	0	20
Manchester City	08.64	14	0	1
Aston Villa	11.64	45	0	18
Shrewsbury Town	10.67	34	2	9

STOWELL Michael
Portsmouth	19 April 1965			
Preston North End	02.85	0	0	0
Everton	12.85	0	0	0
Chester City (L)	09.87	14	0	0
York City (L)	12.87	6	0	0
Manchester City (L)	02.88	14	0	0
Port Vale (L)	10.88	7	0	0
Wolverhampton Wands (L)	03.89	7	0	0
Preston North End (L)	02.90	2	0	0
Wolverhampton Wands	06.90	359	0	0

SUCKLING Perry J.
Leyton	12 October 1965			
Coventry City	10.83	27	0	0
Manchester City	06.86	39	0	0
Crystal Palace	01.88	59	0	0
West Ham United (L)	12.89	6	0	0
Brentford (L)	10.91	8	0	0
Watford	07.92	4	0	0
Doncaster Rovers	07.94	30	0	0

SUGRUE Paul A.
Coventry	6 November 1960			
Manchester City	02.80	5	1	0
Cardiff City	08.81	2	3	0
Middlesbrough	12.82	66	3	6
Portsmouth	12.84	2	2	0
Northampton Town	03.86	2	6	2
Newport County	08.86	1	1	0

SUMMERBEE Michael G.
Cheltenham	15 December 1942			

The Blues

Niall Quinn

Spotted by Arsenal playing junior football in the Republic of Ireland with Manortown United, he made his first team debut for the Gunners in December 1985, scoring a goal in a 2-0 win over Liverpool. With Arsenal he won a League Cup winners' medal in 1987 and made the first of 69 appearances for the Republic of Ireland. However, after the Gunners had signed Alan Smith, Quinn's first team opportunities became less and he found himself languishing in the reserves. He was eventually rescued from obscurity when signing for Manchester City in March 1990. He marked his debut for the Blues with a goal in a 1-1 draw against Chelsea and three more strikes by the end of the season secured his place in the Irish World Cup squad for Italy. He missed just one game in 1990-91 as City climbed to fifth place in Division One, scoring his first hat-trick for the club in a 3-1 win at Crystal Palace.

Very few forwards cause more havoc in the air than Quinn and this coupled with his fantastic work-rate and neat distribution and the superb way he holds up the ball have made him into one of the best forwards in Europe, At Maine Road, Quinn averaged a goal every third game but during the 1996 close season he left to join Sunderland for £1.3 million, the Wearsiders' record signing.

After a number of impressive performances in the early part of the 1996-97 season, he damaged an ankle which kept him out of first team action for seven months. It looked as though the popular Irishman was going to miss the bulk of the 1997-98 season as well following a third knee operation in a year. However he returned to first team action in November 1997 and formed a prolific partnership with Kevin Phillips. Having scored the first goal at the Stadium of Light in a 3-1 win over Manchester City he went on to score 14 league goals including a hat-trick in a 4-1 win over Stockport County. He also scored twice in the play-off final at Wembley which Sunderland lost 7-6 on penalties after drawing 4-4 with Charlton Athletic. In 1998-99, when Sunderland won the First Division Championship, Quinn was in outstanding form and took his tally of goals for the Wearsiders to 41 in 98 games.

bananas appeared on the Maine Road terraces, helping the Blues to six successive victories just after the turn of the year. As the season neared its close, City began to feel the pressure and on 29 April found themselves 2-0 down at half-time to Oxford United. A tremendous second-half performance saw the Blues turn the game round to win 4-2. There were just three games remaining, the first against fellow-promotion contenders Crystal Palace. Nigel Gleghorn gave City an early lead but then had to go in goal after Andy Dibble failed to come out for the second-half following an earlier injury. Gleghorn performed heroics and though Ian Wright equalised for the Eagles, City hung on to draw 1-1. After a 3-3 home draw against Bournemouth, the Blues travelled to Bradford City needing just a point for promotion. The Yorkshire side went a goal up after 24 minutes whilst promotion rivals Crystal Palace were 4-0 up against Birmingham City. The Maine Road faithful urged on their side but it looked like a lost cause as the final whistle approached. There were just four minutes remaining when Tony Morley netted the equaliser that meant City were back in the First Division.

That season's Cup competitions saw City lose 3-1 to Brentford in the fourth round of the FA Cup after beating Leicester City 1-0. In the Littlewoods Cup, City beat Plymouth Argyle 7-3 on aggregate after a remarkable 6-3 win at Home Park in the second-leg before a Paul Moulden hat-trick helped them beat Sheffield United 4-2. The Blues went out of the competition in the next round, losing 3-1 at Luton Town.

The club's opening match in the top flight in 1989-90 was at Anfield and not surprisingly they went down 3-1 to the Merseysiders. The club's two summer

SwindonTown	03.60	218	0	39
Manchester City	08.65	355	2	47
Burnley	06.75	51	0	0
Blackpool	12.76	3	0	0
Stockport County	08.77	86	1	6

SUMMERBEE Nicholas J.

Altrincham	26 August 1971			
SwindonTown	07.89	89	23	6
Manchester City	06.94	119	12	6
Sunderland	11.97	58	3	6

SWIFT Frank V.

Blackpool	26 December 1913			
Manchester City	10.32	338	0	0

SYMONS Christopher J.

Basingstoke	8 March 1971			
Portsmouth	12.88	161	0	10
Manchester City	08.95	124	0	4
Fulham	07.98	450	1	1

TAGGART Gerald P.

Belfast	18 October 1970			
Manchester City	07.89	10	2	1
Barnsley	01.90	209	3	16
Bolton Wanderers	08.95	68	1	4
Leicester City	07.98	9	6	0

TAYLOR Kenneth V.

Manchester	18 June 1936			
Manchester City	08.54	1	0	0

TELFORD William A.

Carlisle	5 March 1956			
Manchester City	08.75	0	1	0
Peterborough United	09.75	3	1	2
Colchester United (L)	01.76	1	1	1

THOMAS Scott L.

Bury	30 October 1974			
Manchester City	03.92	0	2	0
Brighton & Hove Alb (L)	03.98	7	0	0

THOMPSON George H.

Maltby	15 September 1926			
Chesterfield	06.47	0	0	0
Scunthorpe United	06.50	92	0	0
Preston North End	10.52	140	0	0
Manchester City	06.56	2	0	0
Carlisle United	06.57	202	0	0

THOMPSTONE Ian P.

Bury	17 July 1971			
Manchester City	07.89	0	1	1

The Blues

signings Clive Allen and Ian Bishop impressed but it was to be the fifth game of the season before they were on a winning side, City beating Queen's Park Rangers 1-0. After losing their next game at Wimbledon came the first Manchester derby game for three years because the teams had been playing in different divisions. City went ahead in the 11th minute through David Oldfield and then extended their lead within a matter of seconds when Tony Morley fired home after his first shot had been saved by Jim Leighton. The Blues scored a third goal nine minutes from half-time wen Bishop headed in an inch-perfect cross from Oldfield. Early in the second-half Mark Hughes pulled a goal back for United with a superb bicycle kick but further goals from Oldfield and Hinchcliffe saw City run out winners 5-1 to record their biggest 'derby' win at Maine Road !

After beating Luton in their next game, City won only one of their next ten league matches, suffering three heavy defeats against Arsenal (Away 0-4) Derby County (Away 0-6) and Liverpool (Home 1-4). In November 1989, Mel Machin gave way to Ken Barnes and Tony Book, who ran the team on a temporary basis until the arrival of new manager Howard Kendall the following month. His first game in charge was at his former club Everton and City, who were bottom of the table, secured a point in a goalless draw. Two players who made their debuts in this match were player-coach Peter Reid and Alan Harper, both of whom played under Kendall during his time as Everton manager. The year ended with wins over Norwich City and Millwall before City later drew 1-1 with Manchester United at Old Trafford with Ian Brightwell scoring for the Blues. City were still languishing near the foot

of the table but four successive wins in the last 11 matches, of which only one was lost, helped the club end the campaign in 14th place.

After losing their opening game of the 1990-91 season, 3-1 at Tottenham Hotspur, City embarked on an unbeaten 10-match run which took the club into the top five. One of these matches was the Maine Road derby against Manchester United which ended all-square at 3-3 with David White (2) and Colin Hendry the City scorers. After the Blues' next game, a 1-1 draw at Sunderland, Howard Kendall returned to Everton to manage his old club. Peter Reid was named as the club's new player-manager and under his guidance, City moved steadily up the table. In April the club embarked on a seven-match unbeaten run which included victories over Derby County (Home 2-1) and Aston Villa (Away 5-1). The Derby encounter saw Niall Quinn make history by scoring for City at one end and then saving Dean Saunders'

Tony Coton

Goalkeeper Tony Coton joined Birmingham City from local non-League side Mile Oak Rovers of Tamworth and made a sensational start in his Football League debut at home to Sunderland in December 1980 when he saved a penalty after less than a minute !

He became a regular in the Birmingham side in 1982-83 but after 114 appearances for the St Andrew's club, he joined Watford early into the 1984-85 season. He immediately replaced Steve Sherwood and soon became a big favourite at Vicarage Road being voted 'Player of the Year' on three separate occasions.

He was transferred to Manchester City for £1 million in the summer of 1990 and after replacing Andy Dibble helped the Blues to finish in fifth place in Division One. His performances that season took him into the England reckoning yet his only international honour was as a substitute in an England 'B' match in 1991-92. He appeared in 194 games for the Maine Road club before moving across the city to join Manchester United. Having failed to break into the club's first team, he left to join Sunderland in July 1996. After only 10 appearances in the Premier League he was involved in an accidental collision with then Southampton striker Egil Ostenstad and fractured his leg in five places.

Oldham Athletic	05.90	0	0	0
Exeter City	01.92	15	0	3
Halifax Town	07.92	31	0	9
Scunthorpe United	03.93	47	13	8
Rochdale	07.95	11	14	1
Scarborough	08.96	12	7	2
Bury	03.97	0	0	0

THURLOW Alec C.E.

Depwade	24 February 1922			
Huddersfield Town	09.44	0	0	0
Manchester City	09.46	21	0	0

TIATTO Daniele A.

Melbourne, Australia	22 May 1973			
Stoke City (L)	11.97	11	4	1
Manchester City	07.98	8	9	0

TOLMIE James

Glasgow	20 November 1960			
Manchester City	08.83	46	15	15
Carlisle United	03.86	7	1	1

TOWERS Anthony M.

Manchester	13 April 1952			
Manchester City	04.69	117	5	10
Sunderland	03.74	108	0	18
Birmingham City	07.77	90	2	4
Rochdale (N/C)	02.85	1	1	0

TRACEY Simon P.

Woolwich	9 December 1967			
Wimbledon	02.86	1	0	0
Sheffield United	10.88	203	3	0
Manchester City (L)	10.94	3	0	0
Norwich City	12.94	1	0	0
Wimbledon (L)	11.95	1	0	0

TRAUTMANN Bernhard C.

Germany	22 October 1923			
Manchester City	11.49	508	0	0

TSKHADADZE Kakhaber

Rustavi, Georgia	7 September 1968			
Manchester City	02.98	12	0	2

TUEART Dennis

Newcastle	27 November 1949			
Sunderland	08.67	173	5	46
Manchester City	03.74	139	1	59
Manchester City	02.80	77	7	27
Stoke City	08.83	2	1	0
Burnley	12.83	8	7	5

The Blues

Uwe Rösler

East German international Uwe Rösler joined the Blues from Dynamo Dresden for £750,000 in March 1994 and made his debut in a 1-1 draw at Queen's Park Rangers. He scored five goals in his 12 appearances at the end of that season to help the club retain its Premier League status. The following season Rösler was the club's leading scorer with 15 league goals and netted four in a 5-2 League Cup win over Notts County. Though he was unable to show the same level of consistency in 1995-96 he demonstrated his ability to create something out of nothing when he scored against Manchester United in the 3-2 defeat at Maine Road. That season he formed a good understanding with Paul Walsh but thereafter playing under a number of different managers he was left to forage alone with little support. After three seasons at Maine Road as the club's leading goalscorer and a firm favourite with the City fans, he began the 1997-98 season by refusing to sign a new contract and was made available for transfer. Though he was hampered by injuries he took his tally of goals scored for City to 64 in 177 League and Cup games before signing a three-year contract with Kaiserslautern and left Maine Road on a free transfer.

penalty after he had replaced Tony Coton in goal, who had been sent-off for dragging down Derby's Welsh international centre-forward. In City's victory at Villa Park, David White became the first Maine Road player since the war to score four goals in an away match. This run of undefeated matches came to an end in the penultimate game of the season in the Old Trafford derby. City lost 1-0 with Colin Hendrey deflecting Ryan Giggs' shot past the club's young debutant 'keeper Martyn Margetson. The Blues ended the campaign in fifth place after beating Sunderland 3-2 in the final game of the season.

During the summer of 1991, City broke their record transfer fee when they splashed out £2.5 million on Wimbledon's Keith Curle. Immediately appointed captain, Curle and his men won their opening three games of the season to go top of the table. Despite losing three successive games in September, City then won five and drew three of their next nine matches, including four victories on the trot. Then after losing 3-1 at Aston Villa, the Blues embarked on another unbeaten run, this time of eight matches to remain in the top three. One player who joined City during the course of the season was Steve McMahon from Liverpool for a fee of £900,000 and it was he who inspired the club during this period. After losing their way somewhat in February, City lost three games in succession in March before beating Championship favourites Leeds United at Maine Road 4-0. The club's next game was the Old Trafford derby in which a Keith Curle penalty earned City a point. The Blues won their last four games of the season with top-scorer David White netting a hat-trick on the final day as City beat Oldham Athletic 5-

TURNBULL Ronald W.
Newbiggin	18 July 1922			
Sunderland	11.47	40	0	16
Manchester City	09.49	30	0	5
Swansea City	01.51	67	0	35

VANBLERK Jason
Sydney, Australia	16 March 1968			
Millwall	09.94	68	5	2
Manchester City	08.97	10	9	0
West Bromwich Albion	03.98	38	0	0

VARADI Imre
Paddington	8 July 1959			
Sheffield United	04.78	6	4	4
Everton	03.79	22	4	6
Newcastle United	08.81	81	0	39
Sheffield Wednesday	08.83	72	4	33
West Bromwich Albion	07.85	30	2	9
Manchester City	10.86	56	9	26
Sheffeild Wednesday	09.88	14	8	3
Leeds United	02.90	19	3	4
Luton Town (L)	03.92	5	1	1
Oxford United (L)	01.93	3	2	0
Rotherham United	03.93	55	12	25
Mansfield Town	08.95	1	0	0
Scunthorpe United	09.95	0	2	0

VAUGHAN Anthony J.
Manchester	11 October 1975			
Ipswich Town	07.94	56	11	3
Manchester City	07.97	54	3	2

VILJOEN Colin
South Africa	20 June 1948			
Ipswich Town	03.67	303	2	45
Manchester City	08.78	25	2	0
Chelsea	03.80	19	1	0

VONK Michel C.
Alkmaar, Holland	28 October 1968			
Manchester City	03.92	87	4	3
Oldham Athletic (L)	11.95	5	0	1
Sheffield United	12.95	37	0	2

WAGSTAFFE David
Manchester	5 April 1943			
Manchester City	05.60	144	0	8
Wolverhampton Wands	12.64	324	0	27
Blackburn Rovers	01.76	72	3	7
Blackpool	08.78	17	2	1
Blackburn Rovers	03.79	2	0	0

The Blues

2 at Boundary Park. This excellent end to the season once again enabled City to finish fifth in the League.

Following reorganisation during the summer, City began the 1992-93 season in the newly formed Premier League. One of a number of new players to join the club was Terry Phelan, who on signing from Wimbledon for £2. 5 million became the most expensive full-back in British soccer. The club's first game in the Premier League saw them draw 1-1 at home to Queen's Park Rangers with David White scoring the City goal. After two successive away defeats, City won three and drew one of their next four games with David White scoring in each of those games. In fact, White scored 11 goals in the first 15 matches which earned him an England call-up. City lost their next three matches and then drew two before embarking on a run of four successive victories in which Mike Sheron found the net in each of those successes. Sheron vindicated Peter Reid's faith in his ability by scoring some important goals as the season unfolded. Results over the rest of the campaign were mixed and this was due in the main to an injury crisis - Paul Lake suffering a recurrence of a serious knee problem and David Brightwell, Andy Hill and Ian Brightwell all missing a good number of games. One of the finds of the season was Garry Flitcroft, his powerful performances in midfield helping the club to end the campaign in nith place. That season's FA Cup saw City reach the quarter-finals with wins over Reading (Away 4-0 after a 1-1 draw) Queen's Park Rangers (Away 2-1) and Barnsley (Home 2-0). Their opponents at Maine Road were Tottenham Hotspur. The Blues went down 4-2 but the game was marred by a pitch invasion which cost the club a

large fine and an FA reprimand.

For many, the 1993-94 season will be remembered for the events which took place in the boardroom rather than on the pitch. After City had drawn one and lost three of their opening four games, Chairman Peter Swales responded by bringing in journalist John Maddocks as the club's general manager. Within six days of Maddock's appointment, Peter Reid was shown the door and replaced by Oxford United manager, Brian Horton. Despite the club winning three of its four games in September, the fans were still unsettled and demanded that Swales should leave Maine Road, especially when it became known that former City favourite Francis Lee was considering trying to take over the club. In the derby game against United at Maine Road in early November, City led 2-0 before going down 3-2.

On 29 November 1993, Peter Swales decided to step down as chairman but Francis Lee and his consortium had lengthy negotiations to conduct before they could take over. The situation on the playing side wasn't helped when a serious injury to the Republic of Ireland international Niall Quinn ruled him out for the rest of the season. Francis Lee eventually took control by paying £3 million for 30% of the shares. The team responded by beating Ipswich Town 2-1 with goals from Griffiths and Flitcroft. A number of new players arrived at Maine Road to help the club's fight against relegation: Peter Beagrie from Everton; David Rocastle from Leeds United; Paul Walsh from Portsmouth and Uwe Rösler and Stefan Karl from Germany. Though they took a little time to settle, they helped City to win three and draw seven of their last 12 matches, enabling the Blues to end their second season of

Premiership football in 16th place.

After being beaten 3-0 at Arsenal on the opening day of the 1994/95 season, City bounced back with emphatic 3-0 and 4-0 wins over West Ham United and Everton at Maine Road. City took just one point from their next three away games before beating Queen's Park Rangers 2-1 at Loftus Road. It was a remarkable performance as the Blues ended the game with just nine men, Andy Dibble and Richard Edghill having been sent-off ! The club's home form was very impressive but on 10 November 1994, the Blues were beaten 5-0 at Old Trafford as Andrei Kanchelskis scored the first derby hat-trick since Francis Lee's treble in 1970. Despite this setback, City responded with three straight wins which took Brian Horton's side up to sixth place in the Premier League. However, the next game saw City lose their unbeaten home record, when Arsenal won 2-1 to complete the 'double' over the Maine Road club. The Blues then embarked on a 10-match run without a win including losing 3-0 at home to Manchester United. There was a slight revival over Easter as City beat Liverpool 2-1 at home and Blackburn Rovers 3-2 at Ewood Park but after the club picked up just two points from the last four games they slipped down to end the season in 17th place.

In that season's League Cup, City lost 1-0 at Barnet but two goals from Niall Quinn helped the Blues win the second leg 4-1 to go through to a third round meeting with Queen's Park Rangers. City found themselves a goal behind after just 15 seconds but fought back well to win the Loftus Road encounter 4-3. They then beat Newcastle United 2-0 at St James Park after the first meeting at Maine Road had ended all-square at 1-1. City's form after the turn of the year dipped and in the fifth round match at

WALSH Michael T.

Manchester	20 June 1956			
Bolton Wanderers	07.74	169	8	4
Everton	08.81	20	0	0
Norwich City (L)	10.82	5	0	0
Burnley (L)	12.82	3	0	0
Manchester City	10.83	3	1	0
Blackpool	02.84	146	7	5
Bury	07.89	0	0	0

WALSH Paul A.

Plumstead	1 October 1962			
Charlton Athletic	10.79	85	2	24
LutonTown	07.82	80	0	24
Liverpool	05.84	63	14	25
Tottenham Hotspur	02.88	88	44	19
Queen's Park Rangers (L)	09.91	2	0	0
Portsmouth	06.92	67	6	14
Manchester City	03.94	53	0	16
Portsmouth	09.95	21	0	5

WALSH William

Dublin	31 May 1921			
Manchester City	06.38	109	0	1

WARD Ashley S.

Manchester	24 November 1970			
Manchester City	08.89	0	1	0
Wrexham (L)	01.91	4	0	2
Leicester City	07.91	2	8	0
Blackpool (L)	11.92	2	0	1
Crewe Alexandra	12.92	58	32	5
Norwich City	12.94	53	0	18
Derby County	03.96	32	8	9
Barnsley	09.97	45	12	0
Blackburn Rovers	12.98	17	0	5

WARD Mark W.

Huyton	10 October 1962			
Everton	09.80	0	0	0
Oldham Athletic	07.83	84	0	12
West Ham United	08.85	163	2	12
Manchester City	12.89	55	0	14
Everton	08.91	82	1	6
Birmingham City	03.94	63	0	7
Huddersfield Town	03.96	7	1	0
Wigan Athletic	09.96	5	0	0

WARHURST Roy

Sheffield	18 September 1926			
Sheffield United	09.44	17	0	2
Birmingham City	03.50	213	0	10
Manchester City	06.57	40	0	2
Crewe Alexandra	03.59	51	0	1
Oldham Athletic	08.60	8	0	0

Georgiou Kinkladze

Georgian international midfielder Georgiou Kinkladze was signed from Dinamo Tbilisi for £2 million at the start of the 1995-96 season and made his debut in a 1-1 draw at home to Tottenham Hotspur on the opening day of the season. That campaign saw him take the Premiership by storm, displaying great skills as he created goalscoring opportunities for himself and his colleagues. His first goal came in the 1-0 win over Aston Villa in November. In 1996-97 Kinkladze reached double figures in terms of goals scored although half of his total came from the penalty-spot. At the end of the season he was elected by his fellow professionals to the PFA award-winning First Division team. Early in the 1997-98 season he was involved in a car crash where he was lucky to walk away without serious injury. Though he continued to score some great goals, perhaps none better than the one against West Ham United in the fourth round of the FA Cup, he seemed to lose form following the appointment of manager Joe Royle. Despite his selection for the City side not being automatic, he continued to score some great goals and at the end of the season in which he had taken his tally to 22 in 121 games he was once again selected for the award-winning PFA First Division team. In May 1998, the little Georgian ended his involvement with English football by signing for Dutch giants, Ajax for £5 million.

WASSALL Darren P.
Birmingham   27 June 1968

Nottingham Forest	06.86	17	10	0
Hereford United (L)	10.87	5	0	0
Bury (L)	03.89	7	0	1
Derby County	06.92	90	8	0
Manchester City (L)	09.96	14	1	0
Birmingham City	03.97	22	3	0

WATSON David V.
Stapleford   5 October 1946

Notts County	01.67	24	1	2
Rotherham United	01.68	121	0	20
Sunderland	12.70	177	0	27
Manchester City	06.75	146	0	4
Southampton	10.79	73	0	7
Stoke City	01.82	59	0	5
Derby County	09.83	34	0	1
Notts County	09.84	23	2	1

WEAVER Nicholas J.
Sheffield   2 March 1979

Mansfield Town	08.96	1	0	0
Manchester City	05.97	45	0	0

WEBSTER Eric
Manchester   24 June 1931

Manchester City	02.52	1	0	0

WESTCOTT Dennis
Wallasey   2 July 1917

New Brighton	01.36	18	0	10
Wolverhampton Wands	07.36	128	0	105
Blackburn Rovers	04.48	63	0	37
Manchester City	02.50	72	0	37
Chesterfield	06.52	40	0	21

WESTWOOD Eric
Manchester   25 September 1917

Manchester City	11.37	248	0	3

WHARTON John E.
Bolton   18 June 1920

Plymouth Argyle	06.37	11	0	2
Preston North End	07.39	25	0	7
Manchester City	03.47	23	0	2
Blackburn Rovers	06.48	129	0	14
Newport County	02.53	740	1	0

WHELAN Anthony M.
Salford   20 November 1952

Manchester United	12.69	0	0	0
Manchester City	03.73	3	3	0
Rochdale	07.74	124	0	20

The Blues

Crystal Palace, the Blues were well beaten 4-0. In the FA Cup, City drew 2-2 at Notts County but in the replay Rösler scored four goals to give the Blues a 5-2 victory. In round four an early goal by Paul Walsh accounted for Aston Villa but in the next round Newcastle gained revenge for their League Cup exit with a 3-1 win.

City's league position led to the departure of Brian Horton and the arrival of Alan Ball as the club's new manager. During the summer, City signed three new players in goalkeeper Eike Immel from VfB Stuttgart, Kit Symons from Portsmouth and Georgian international Georgiou Kinkladze from Dinamo Tbilisi. The 1995-96 season began with Uwe Rösler, top-scorer the previous year, netting an equaliser for City on the opening day against Spurs. Sadly the club lost its next eight Premiership games, including a 1-0 defeat at Old Trafford in the Manchester derby. Another point was gained in a goalless home draw against Leeds United before the Blues were thrashed 6-0 by Liverpool. Anchored firmly to the foot of the Premier League, the club's fortunes took a turn for the better when Nicky Summerbee scored the only goal of the game against Bolton Wanderers. This sparked a run of four wins in five games but sadly City, after losing 4-1 at Middlesbrough, won only three of their next 19 Premiership games. With just three matches to play, the Blues were one place above the relegation positions. Though the Blues beat Sheffield Wednesday and Aston Villa, a number of the other lowly sides also won their games, leaving City really needing to beat Liverpool in the final game to ensure survival. A Maine Road crowd of 31,436, the season's biggest, saw the Blues go in at half-time 2-0 down.

Goals from Rösler and Symons gave some hope but there was no further scoring and City left the field to learn that their comeback had all been in vain, they were relegated on goal difference.

Liverpool also ended City's interest in that season's League Cup competition, beating the Blues 4-0. The FA Cup saw City beat Leicester 5-0 in a replay at Maine Road and after beating Coventry City 2-1, also in a replay, the Blues faced Manchester United in round five. Uwe Rösler netted for City but the Reds won 2-1 to move closer to completing the 'double'. During the close season, there were a number of departures from Maine Road with Niall Quinn, Keith Curle, Terry Phelan, Garry Flitcroft and Tony Coton all moving on to pastures new.

Most of the blame for the club's relegation was directed at Alan Ball and after just three games of the 1996-97 season, he resigned. Asa Hartford took over as caretaker-manager while the board searched for the right man for the job. Their choice was former Manchester United and England winger Steve Coppell, who arrived at the club in early October to find City in 14th place and already knocked out of the League Cup by lowly Lincoln City 5-1 on aggregate. Coppell's reign as manager lasted just 32 days before he too resigned stating that the stress was too much for him.

His assistant Phil Neal took over on a caretaker basis but his first game in charge saw the Blues lose 3-2 at home to Oxford United. The former Liverpool and England defender's term of office ended in defeat at Barnsley at the end of December, a game which chairman Francis Lee missed, being on holiday in Barbados ! The club's new manager was former

Nottingham Forest boss Frank Clark and he inspired the club to embark on a nine-match unbeaten run. Successive victories over Oxford United (Away 4-1) Southend United (Home 3-0) Swindon Town (Home 3-0) and Bradford City (Away 3-1) brought suggestions that perhaps the club could reach the play-offs. However, only four of the final 12 games ended in victory and City finished the season in which they had five managers in 14th place.

The Blues were favourites to win promotion from the First Division in 1997-98 but as things turned out, the club never recovered from a poor start. Having failed to win any of their first four league games and having lost 4-2 on penalties to Second Division Blackpool in the League Cup, City finally won a game when they beat league leaders Nottingham Forest 3-1. Three matches later they demolished another of the early pacesetters, Swindon Town, 6-0 at Maine Road, but it was to be one of only six home wins that season. The club's poor form continued through in to February when Clark was dismissed, learning of his fate through the media. His replacement was former City centre-forward Joe Royle but when he took over the reins, the club were in dire trouble, sitting just one place off the bottom of the table. Sadly Royle could not halt the slide and though the Blues won 5-2 at Stoke City on the final day of the season to send the Potters down, the clubs immediately above the relegation zone also won to send the club into the third fight for the first time in their history. The Blues finished in 22nd place with 48 points - one point and one place short of safety. The disastrous campaign was the last in City shirts for Kinkladze and Rösler and of Francis Lee in the boardroom, the City chairman resigning in the face of

WHITE David

Manchester	30 October 1967			
Manchester City	11.85	273	12	79
Leeds United	12.93	28	14	9
Sheffield United	11.95	55	11	13

WHITE Howard K.

Timperley	2 March 1954			
Manchester City	05.71	1	0	0

WHITFIELD Kenneth

Bishop Auckland	24 March 1930			
Wolverhampton Wands	12.47	9	0	3
Manchester City	03.53	13	0	3
Brighton & Hove Albion	07.54	175	0	4
Queen's Park Rangers	07.59	19	0	3

WHITLEY James

Zambia	14 April 1975			
Manchester City	08.94	27	0	10

WHITLEY Jeffrey

Zambia	28 January 1979			
Manchester City	02.96	27	21	3
Wrexham (L)	01.99	9	0	2

WIEKENS Gerard

Tolhuiswyk, Holland	25 February 1973			
Manchester City	07.97	77	2	7

WILLIAMS Alexander

Manchester	13 November 1961			
Manchester City	11.79	114	0	0
Port Vale	11.86	35	0	0

WILLIAMS Derek

Mold	15 June 1934			
Manchester City	05.51	1	0	0
Wrexham	08.54	12	0	0
Oldham Athletic	09.56	28	0	0

WILLIAMS Eric

Manchester	10 July 1921			
Manchester City	03.45	38	0	0
Halifax Town	10.51	111	0	0

WILLIAMS William R.

Littleborough	7 October 1960			
Rochdale	08.81	89	6	2
Stockport County	07.85	104	0	1
Manchester City	10.88	0	1	0
Stockport County	12.88	171	3	7

condemnation from both fans and shareholders.

The Blues made a good start to the 1998-99 season, beating Blackpool 3-0 in front of a Maine Road crowd of 32,134. Despite losing by the same scoreline at eventual champions Fulham in their next match, City were undefeated in their next nine outings. In the middle of this run, the Blues beat Notts County 7-1 to win 9-1 on aggregate in a first round League Cup tie. Sadly they were knocked out in the next round by Derby County of the Premier League. After beating Wrexham 1-0 at the Racecourse Ground on Boxing Day, City embarked on another unbeaten run, this time of 12 matches and then lost just one of their remaining 11 fixtures to end the season in thirs place, five points adrift of runners-up Walsall, who won automatic promotion to the First Division.

City met Wigan Athletic in the play-off semi-finals and went a goal behind to the Latics after only 20 seconds of the first leg at Springfield Park. Paul Dickov equalised in the 76th minute to make

the final score 1-1. At Maine Road, a Shaun Goater goal separated the teams and took City through to the Wembley final against Gillingham.

They looked dead and buried when second-half goals from Asaba and Taylor left the Kent side on course to reach Division One for the first time in their history. But somehow, the Blues got themsleves together. Kevin Horlock threw them a lifeline when he pulled a goal back in the last minute of normal time. Then in the fourth minute of injury time, Paul Dickov pounced in the box and rifled an unstoppable shot into the roof of the net to complete an amazing fightback. Extra-time failed to separate the sides so it was down to the dreaded penalties, where England Under-21 goalkeeper Nicky Weaver emerged as the hero. He saved Paul Smith's spot-kick and when he kept out Guy Butters' effort, City were up !

Coming four days after Alex Ferguson's side delivered the 90-second phenomenon that shook Europe, City proved that anything United could do, they could do better !

Post War Honours:

First Division Championship Winners: 1967-68
Runners-Up:1976-77

Second Division Championship Winners: 1946-47, 1965-66

FA Cup Winners: 1955-56, 1968-69
Runners-Up: 1954-55, 1980-81

League Cup Winners: 1969-70, 1975-76
League Cup Runners-Up: 1973-74

European Cup Winners Cup Winners: 1969-70

Post War Managers

Wilf Wild: 1932-1946

Sam Cowan: 1946-1947

Jock Thompson: 1947-1950

Les McDowall: 1950-1963

George Poyser: 1963-1965

Joe Mercer OBE: 1965-1972

Malcolm Allison: 1972-1973

Johnny Hart: 1973

Ron Saunders: 1973-1974

Tony Book: 1974-1979

Malcolm Allison: 1979-1980

John Bond: 1980-1983

John Benson: 1983

Billy McNeill MBE: 1983-1986

Jimmy Frizzell: 1986-1987

Mel Machin: 1987-1989

Ken Barnes & Tony Book: 1989

Howard Kendall: 1989-90

Peter Reid: 1990-1993

Brian Horton: 1993-1995

Alan Ball: 1995-1996

Asa Hartford 1996

Steve Coppell: 1996

Phil Neal: 1996

Frank Clarke: 1996-1998

Joe Royle: 1998-

WILLIAMSON John
Manchester   8 May 1929
Manchester City   08.49   59   0   18
Blackburn Rovers   03.56   9   0   3

WILSON Clive A.
Manchester   13 November 1961
Manchester City   12.79   96   2   9
Chester City (L)   09.82   21   0   2
Chelsea   03.87   68   13   5
Manchester City (L)   03.87   11   0   0
Queen's Park Rangers   07.90   170   2   12
Tottenham Hotspur   06.95   67   3   1

WOOD Alfred E.H.
Macclesfield   25 October 1945
Manchester City   06.63   24   1   0
Shrewsbury Town   06.66   257   1   64
Millwall   06.72   91   3   8
Hull City   11.74   51   2   10
Middlesbrough   10.76   22   1   2
Walsall   07.77   26   3   2

WOODROFFE Lewis C.
Portsmouth   29 October 1921
Manchester City   10.45   9   0   1
Watford   08.47   63   0   6

WOOSNAM Philip A.
Caersws   22 December 1932
Manchester City   06.52   1   0   0
Leyton Orient   03.55   108   0   19
West Ham United   11.58   138   0   26
Aston Villa   11.62   106   0   24

WRIGHT Thomas J.
Belfast   29 August 1963
Newcastle United   01.88   72   1   0
Hull City (L)   02.91   6   0   0
Nottingham Forest   09.93   11   0   0
Reading (L)   10.96   17   0   0
Manchester City (L)   01.97   5   0   0
Manchester City   03.97   27   0   0
Wrexham (L)   02.99   16   0   0

YOUNG Neil J.
Manchester   17 February 1944
Manchester City   02.61   332   2   86
Preston North End   01.72   67   1   16
Rochdale   07.74   8   5   4